IMAGES
of Sport

LEICESTERSHIRE
COUNTY CRICKET CLUB

IMAGES
of Sport

LEICESTERSHIRE
COUNTY CRICKET CLUB

Compiled by
Dennis Lambert

TEMPUS

First published 2000
Copyright © Dennis Lambert, 2000

Tempus Publishing Limited
The Mill, Brimscombe Port,
Stroud, Gloucestershire, GL5 2QG

ISBN 0 7524 1864 5

Typesetting and origination by
Tempus Publishing Limited
Printed in Great Britain by
Midway Clark Printing, Wiltshire

Also available from Tempus Publishing

Glamorgan CCC	Andrew Hignell	0 7524 0792 9
Glamorgan CCC 2	Andrew Hignell	0 7524 1137 3
Glamorgan Greats	Andrew Hignell	0 7524 1879 3
Hampshire CCC	Hampshire Cricket Museum	0 7524 1876 9
Kent CCC	William A. Powell	0 7524 1871 9
Scarborough Festival	William A. Powell	0 7524 1638 3
Somerset CCC	Somerset Cricket Museum	0 7524 1585 9
Worcestershire CCC	Les Hatton	0 7524 1834 3
Yorkshire CCC	Mick Pope	0 7524 0756 2
The Five Nations Story	David Hands	0 7524 1851 3

(all books are 128 page softbacks with the exception of *The Five Nations Story* which is a 176 page hardback with colour illustrations.)

Contents

Acknowledgements

My thanks must firstly go to Leicestershire County Cricket Club for allowing me the use of their extensive photograph and print collection, and particularly to Mrs Sylvia Michael, Honorary Archivist at the club, for her kind assistance and advice in the compilation of this book.

Any figures and statistics used comply with the match lists produced by the Association of Cricket Statisticians and Historians. I acknowledge the many copyright owners of the photographs. Neville Chadwick Photography have produced the majority of photographs used. Others include *Leicester Mercury*, *Leicester Evening Mail*, Leicester Photo Co. Ltd, PA News Centre, David Munden Photography, Patrick Eagar, Universal Pictorial Press & Agency Ltd, Fleet Photos, A. Wilkes & Son, Melton Mowbray Times Co. Ltd, and Sport and General Press Agency Ltd. My apologies are offered to anyone whose photographs have been used inadvertently without acknowledgement.

Thank you also to David Buxton and James Howarth of Tempus Publishing for their advice and assistance during the compilation and to Charles Palmer CBE for agreeing to write the foreword. Finally, to the late Eric Snow, my mentor and friend for many years, for his encouragement and instruction, without which my knowledge of the history of the Leicestershire County Cricket Club would have been meagre.

Bibliography

E.E. Snow, *A History of Leicestershire Cricket* (Backus, 1949); E.E. Snow, *Leicestershire Cricket, 1949 to 1977* (Stanley Paul, 1977); E.E. Snow, *Country House Cricket Grounds of Leicestershire and Rutland* (ACS, 1998); D.A. Lambert, *The History of Leicestershire County Cricket Club* (Helm, 1992); D.A. Lambert, *Leicestershire Cricketers 1879-1977* (ACS, 1977); D.A. Lambert, *Leicestershire County Cricket Club First-Class Records 1894-1996* (Limlow,1997); E.E. Snow, *Cricket Grounds of Leicestershire* (ACS, 1987); Bailey, Thorn, and Wynne-Thomas, *Who's Who of Cricketers* (Hamlyn, 1993); W.H. Frindall, *England Test Cricketers* (Collins Willow, 1989); P. Wynne-Thomas, *England On Tour* (Hamlyn, 1982); Wisden Cricketers' Almanack (various years); Leicestershire CCC Year Book (various years); ACS International Cricket Year Book (various years). The following periodicals were also consulted: *Cricket*, *The Cricketer*, *Playfair Cricket Monthly*, *Wisden Cricket Monthly*, *The Cricket Statistician*.

Foreword

I think that this is a little gem of a book. It does not lecture you but just prints photographs and provides captions on which readers can hang their own reactions. I think any supporter of Leicestershire will find many ways of bringing the pictures to life.

I have been fortunate in having such a long and close connection with Leicestershire that I can 'see behind' many of the still pictures. For example p. 99 shows Graham Mackenzie, a fine gentle giant of a man, and a great fast bowler. He was one of a party of Leicestershire players invited by Bill Bentley – the then president – to his sumptuously appointed house on his farm. Coming from an enjoyable party we were perturbed to see Graham limping. His response to our concern was, 'Oh, I just fell off the president's carpet!'

I feel greatly satisfied that the book has helped to fill many a gap in my knowledge. I was fascinated by the sections 'Early Days' and 'The Formation of the Club'. I have also enjoyed being reminded of great individual performances such as that of J.H. King (p. 31) who, while on the ground-staff of MCC, was drafted in as a replacement for an absentee from the Gentlemen versus Players match in 1904. He scored a century for the Players in each innings (unrepeated since) and, *mirabile dictu*, he scored a double century against Hampshire when he was fifty-two!

Photographs of Aubrey Sharp and George Gearey (p. 41) reminded me of them in the committee room at Grace Road in the full flow of reminiscence – perhaps only possible when they were well into the 'sere and yellow' and thus impregnable against anyone who tried to interrupt or contradict!

I also rejoiced to see praised such a friend and contemporary as Maurice Tompkin, who died so young at thirty-seven. He was senior pro when I was captain, and no captain could have been better favoured – any dressing-room problems were solved in Maurice's easy way, long before they could reach me.

From the simple contents of the book, I feel I could have written a foreword three times as long as the book itself, but anymore now would, I fear, be sheer indulgence.

Dennis Lambert and Sylvia Michael deserve our sincere thanks and congratulations – they say it was a labour of love. It has certainly been a joy to write the foreword to a book which we hope will be widely accepted.

Introduction

The first match played by Leicestershire – as the county rather than the town or club – took place at Burley, the private ground of the Earls of Winchilsea, in 1791. The game was against the MCC, who were the winners by an innings. George Finch, the Ninth Earl of Winchilsea, played for the visitors. In the July of the following year, Nottinghamshire v. Leicestershire and Rutland was one match of a cricket week at Burley. Both Leicestershire and Nottinghamshire had a large hosiery industry, based on framework knitters working from their homes. This way of life, giving flexibility of working hours compared with other manufacturing industries or agricultural labour, enabled them to practice their cricket. In turn, this led to a great rivalry between the two counties on the cricket field.

A Leicester Club was formed in 1780, playing on St Margaret's Pasture, and two matches with Nottingham in the early part of that decade ended in bickering and dispute, with the result that there were no further meetings for some years. This club appears to have collapsed around 1818. A new club was formed, which laid out the Wharf Street ground in Leicester, and the first match was played at this venue in 1825. With the rapid development of the town, Wharf Street fell prey to the builders in 1860. During the 1860s Leicestershire teams played at various grounds around the county – these were mostly versus the touring All England and United All England elevens. Between 1872 and 1877, county matches took place at Victoria Park in Leicester, which was principally used as a racecourse. At this time, county matches were organised and the teams chosen by the Leicester Cricket Club Committee and the Leicestershire Cricket Association.

The Leicestershire Cricket Ground Company was formed in 1877 to purchase land at Grace Road to lay out a cricket ground. This took place in 1877, and the venue was ready for use in the following summer. The first Australians were met in July 1878, and they won the match by eight wickets. The Leicestershire County Cricket Club was formed on 25 March 1879, and thus the current club came into being. The Sixth Earl of Lanesborough was elected as the first president. The county was not then first-class, but during the 1880s played some of the major counties with varying degrees of success. Surrey were beaten at Grace Road in 1886 by ten wickets and, two years later, the Australians were defeated by 20 runs.

At the MCC Annual General Meeting on 2 May 1894, Derbyshire, Warwickshire, Essex, and Leicestershire were admitted to 'first-class' status, Hampshire following them in 1895. Leicestershire began their first-class career against Essex at Leyton on 14 May 1894, winning the match by 68 runs. The match was a personal triumph for Dick Pougher, who scored a century and took 14 wickets. The county followed this up by beating Yorkshire, and then MCC, but only won two more matches that first season. Their first season in the County Championship was in 1895, when again they started well, but tailed off drastically, finishing twelfth out of fourteen. The move to Aylestone Road took place for the beginning of the 1901 season. Up to the beginning of the First World War, the highest positions Leicestershire had obtained in the County Championship were seventh in 1904 and fifth in 1905. These were hard times, but they never actually finished bottom of the table!

After the war, and throughout the 1920s, on the field Leicestershire were virtually carried by the two all-rounders, George Geary and Ewart Astill. Leslie Berry commenced his long career in 1924, but he did not really come into prominence until the next decade. There was a spell, between 1927 and 1929, when the county came seventh, ninth, and ninth respectively, and later sixth in 1935 – when Ewart Astill became Leicestershire's first appointed professional captain. Otherwise their days were spent in the lower reaches of the Championship. The Aylestone Road ground was occupied by the National Fire Service almost as soon as war broke out in 1939, and after the war it was taken over by Leicester Corporation. Leicestershire returned to Grace Road in 1946, on a temporary tenure from the Leicester Education Committee, the then owners of the ground. The freehold was not to be acquired until January 1966.

Leicestershire's mercurial traits now became even more evident. Leslie Berry captained the county for the first three seasons after the Second World War, and they achieved reasonable positions, before plummeting to the bottom in 1949, improving by one place in each of the next two. Sixth position in 1952 became third – the highest ever at the time – the following season. In 1954, a very wet season, they dropped to sixteenth. After a better 1955, for the next ten seasons Leicestershire were only twice above the bottom four. Tony Lock's three years in charge brought an improvement, with another third place in 1967. Then came Ray Illingworth. Two very modest seasons were followed by a steady rise, culminating in the winning of the County Championship at long last in 1975. The groundwork had been completed, the self-belief was there, and whilst individual players have come and gone, since then Leicestershire have only fallen below tenth place in three seasons. The County Championship was won again in 1996 and 1998, together with the Benson & Hedges Cup in 1972, 1975 and 1985.

This book has been put together – with the enthusiastic help of Mrs Sylvia Michael, Committee Member and Honorary Archivist of the Leicestershire County Cricket Club – entirely from photographs in the club's collection. I have tried to present it as a social history and to portray events and personalities off, as well as on, the field of play. It has been a labour of love.

Dennis Lambert
March 2000

One
Early Days

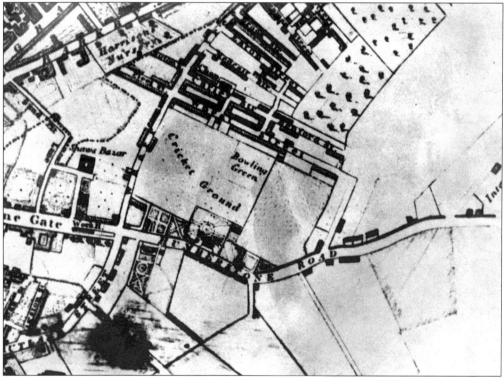

The new ground was completed in 1825, and the opening match was between the County Club and the Rest of Leicester on 25 June. Many other forms of entertainment also took place there. The most important match played at Wharf Street was North *v.* South in September 1836, when Alfred Mynn made 125 not out despite sustaining a serious injury to his leg before the game started. The ground was sold in 1860 and within a few years all trace of it had disappeared under shops and houses.

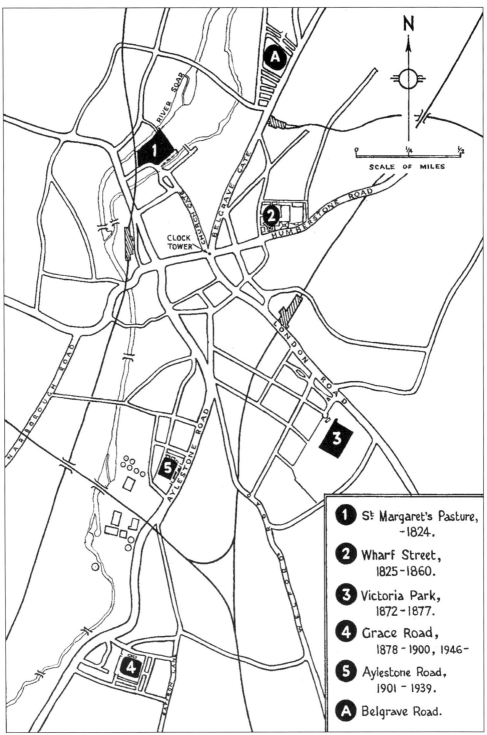

1 Sᵗ Margaret's Pasture, -1824.

2 Wharf Street, 1825-1860.

3 Victoria Park, 1872-1877.

4 Grace Road, 1878-1900, 1946-

5 Aylestone Road, 1901-1939.

A Belgrave Road.

St Margaret's Pasture ground still exists as a sports centre whilst Victoria Park is still used by local clubs. Belgrave Cricket and Cycle Ground had only a short life, between 1880 and 1901, and was then built over.

Note that 'Nottingham' was actually the Sherwood Forest Club, and the game was played on their ground for 200 sovereigns. This match is not recorded in *Scores and Biographies*. The Leicester County Club was formed to lay out and operate the new Wharf Street ground but, like many clubs of the time, was short-lived and disappeared after 1829.

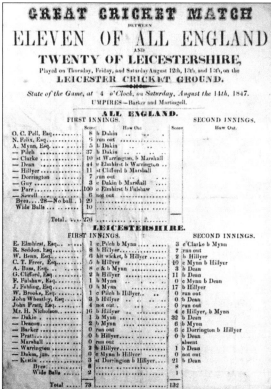

The All England XI was formed by William Clarke of Nottingham in 1846, and for some twenty years matches played by this itinerant band were very popular – perhaps more so than county matches. Their strength was such that XX of Leicestershire were easily defeated at Wharf Street by an innings and 71 runs. The century maker, George Parr, known as 'The Lion of the North', was undoubtedly the best batsman in the country during the late 1840s and throughout the 1850s.

Richard Arthur Henry Mitchell was born at Enderby Hall in Leicester on 22 January 1843. An Etonian, he got his blue at Oxford each year from 1862 to 1865, and was captain in the last three. He also played for Leicestershire between 1860 and 1874, although becoming an assistant master at Eton in 1866 restricted his appearances on the cricket field. A hard-hitting batsman and medium-paced round-arm bowler, he also made 10 stumpings in first-class cricket.

The motley garb worn by the players in this photograph is indicative of local cricket of the time – note the well worn pads. Victoria Park was the local racecourse until 1883, and the cricket ground was laid in the centre. For this reason it was known as the Racecourse Ground. The two-storey pavilion was severely damaged by a German land-mine in 1940. There is now a new structure in a different area of the ground.

Victoria Park Cricket Ground, Leicester.

GRAND CRICKET MATCH

BETWEEN THE

United South of England C.C. and 22 of Leicester & District.

ON MONDAY, TUESDAY, & WEDNESDAY, JULY 15, 16, & 17, 1872.

South of England Eleven.	First Innings.		Second Innings	
W. G. Grace, Esq.	b. Bishop	23	c. Hurst, b. Panter ..	26
Mr. Charlwood	c. Crofts, b. Bishop	11	b C. Randon	1
G. F Grace, Esq.	c. Hurst, b. Bishop ...	7	b. F. Randon	0
Mr. T. Humphrey	c. F. Randon, b. Bishop	17	c Freer, b. Bishop ...	1
„ Lillywhite	c. and b. Bishop	0	c. Fox, b. Bishop ...	0
„ H. H. Stephenson ...	b. Bishop	2	c. Collier, b Panter .	9
„ Caffyn	c. Freer, b. Bishop ...	1	b. F Randon ...	20
„ Fillery	c. Warren, b. Bishop ...	5	not out	2
„ Reed	c. Warren, b. F. Randon	6	c. Hurst, b. Panter .	0
„ Galpin	c. Bishop, b. F. Randon	3	b. Panter . ..	0
„ Phillips	not out	0	c. Buswell, b. F. Randon	4
			Extra	1
	Total	75	Total . .	64

Leicester and District.	First Innings.		Second Innings.	
Mr. A. W. Crofts	st. Phillips, b. Lillywhite	0	b. Galpin ..	1
„ G. Allen	c. Phillips, b. Lillywhite	6	l.b.w., b. Grace	4
„ C. H. Brunt	b. Galpin	1	c. Reed, b. W. G. Grace	0
„ G. Panter	b. Lillywhite	4	c. and b. W. G. Grace ..	23
„ E. Hurst	l.b.w., b. Lillywhite	9	c. Phillips, b. Fillery ..	9
„ T. E. Warren	c. Phillips, b. Galpin ...	2	not out	2
„ G. Bishop	c. Stephenson, b. Lillywhite	0	c. Phillips, b. W. G. Grace	0
„ F. W. Gardiner ...	c. W. G. Grace, b. Galpin	0	c. and b. W. G. Grace .	1
„ A. Buswell	c. G. F. Grace, b. Galpin	12	c. and b. Fillery ..	6
„ J. Collier	c. W.G.Grace, b. Lillywhite	10	st. Phillips, b. W. G. Grace	1
„ J. D. Harris	c. Reed, b. Lillywhite ..	1	b. Fillery ..	0
„ F Randon	b Galpin	8	c. and b. Fillery .	0
„ H. Walter	st. Phillips, b. Lillywhite	2	c. Reed, b W. G. Grace	4
„ E. Holmes	b. Galpin	1	b. W. G Grace .	0
„ A. J Hamel	c. W. G. Grace, b. Llwhite	0	b. W. G. Grace .	0
„ F. Condon	ht. wkt., b. Lillywhite...	0	c. Lillywhite, b. W.G.Grace	0
„ T. Pollard	b. Lillywhite	3	b. Fillery ..	1
„ W. E. Death	c Charlwood, b. Llwhite	0	c. Caffyn, b. W. G. Grace	4
„ C. Randon...	c. W. G. Grace, b Galpin	0	b. Fillery	0
„ J. Timson	not out	0	b. W. G. Grace .	0
„ J. L Freer	c. W. G. Grace, b. Galpin	2	b. W. G. Grace	0
„ W. H. Fox	b. Galpin	2	c. and b. W. G. Grace ..	0
	Extras	5		
	Total	68	Total ...	56

BOWLING ANALYSIS.

1st Innings.—11 U.S.E.					2nd Innings.—11 U.S.E.			
	Overs.	Maidns.	Runs.	Wkts.		Overs.	Maidns.	Runs.	Wkts.
Bishop .. .	41	21	40	8	Bishop ..	24	15	19	2
F. Randon ..	20	7	14	2	C. Randon	15	7	18	1
Panter	20	7	21	0	Panter ..	18 2 bls.	10	14	4
					F. Randon	12	6	12	3

1st Innings —22 L. & D.					2nd Innings.—22 L. & D.			
Lillywhite ..	47	29	31	12	W G. Grace..	34 2 b s 19		35	14
Galpin .	47	27	32	9	Galpin ..	11	7	6	1
					Fillery ..	23	16	15	6

Umpires : Messrs. Grundy and Mortlock.   *Scorers :* Messrs. F Bassford and M. George.

PRINTED ON THE GROUND BY J. H. BEAZLEY, ALBION STREET, LEICESTER.

The United South of England XI (USEE) was another of the several itinerant elevens playing around the country at the time. Leicestershire cricket was improving, and the USEE only won by 15 runs, despite its strength. Several members of the Leicester XXII played for the present County Club after its formation in 1879.

Leicestershire county matches between 1872 and 1878 were organised and administered by a combination of the Leicester Cricket Club Committee, and the Leicester and Leicestershire Cricket Association. During this period, eleven-a-side matches were played home and away against MCC, Lancashire, Nottinghamshire, Northamptonshire and Bedfordshire, although none of these were first class.

E. Holmes, secretary of the Leicester and Leicestershire Cricket Association, later became president of the County Club, and was also Chief Constable of Leicestershire.

The Leicestershire Cricket Ground Company purchased land from the Duke of Rutland's estate at Grace Road and laid out a cricket ground, together with cycle and running tracks. The ground was ready for use by the late Spring of 1878. Known originally as the 'Aylestone Ground', this is the current county ground. The Athletic Sports programme featured here may well have been the first such meeting held at the new ground.

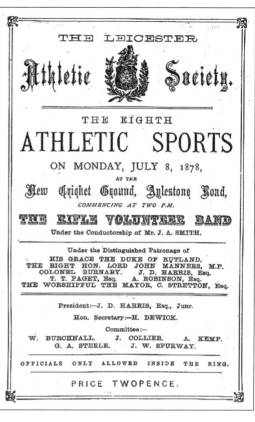

THE LEICESTER

Athletic Society.

THE EIGHTH

ATHLETIC SPORTS

ON MONDAY, JULY 8, 1878,

AT THE

New Cricket Ground, Aylestone Road,

COMMENCING AT TWO P.M.

THE RIFLE VOLUNTEER BAND

Under the Conductorship of Mr. J. A. SMITH.

Under the Distinguished Patronage of

HIS GRACE THE DUKE OF RUTLAND,
THE RIGHT HON. LORD JOHN MANNERS, M.P.
COLONEL BURNABY.   J. D. HARRIS, Esq.
T. T. PAGET, Esq.   A. ROBINSON, Esq.
THE WORSHIPFUL THE MAYOR, C. STRETTON, Esq.

President:—J. D. HARRIS, Esq., Junr.

Hon. Secretary:—H. DEWICK.

Committee:—

W. BURCHNALL.   J. COLLIER.   A. KEMP.
G. A. STEELE.   J. W. SPURWAY.

OFFICIALS ONLY ALLOWED INSIDE THE RING.

PRICE TWOPENCE.

Dan Garner was a well known boot and shoe manufacturer in Leicester. He also ran his own cricket club, known as 'Dan Garner's', which became one of the leading local clubs. Around the turn of the century it was a nursery for the County Club, and many of the young professionals learned their trade there.

The Leicestershire Cricket Ground Company Limited was formed specifically to purchase the land and create the cricket and sports ground at Grace Road. Its initial capital was 2,000 shares of £10 each.

Arnold 'Bobby' Rylott played for Leicestershire between 1875 and 1890, before the county became first class. He joined the ground staff at Lord's in 1872, and played many times for MCC in first-class matches. A fast left-arm bowler, he took 456 wickets in a first-class career lasting from 1870 to 1888. His best performance was 9-30 for MCC *v.* Cambridge University in 1873.

16

The Reverend Edward Elmhirst of Enderby first played for the county in 1842 as a batsmen and wicketkeeper, and was a prominent local player for many years. He represented the Gentlemen v. Players in 1848, scoring 11 and 13. He was rector at Shawell in Leicestershire for fifty-two years and died there in 1893.

The Reverend William 'Tubby' Townshend was born in India in 1849. He was awarded his blue at Oxford from 1870 to 1872, and also played for MCC. Playing for Leicestershire between 1881 and 1885, his highest score was 57 against Uppingham Rovers in his final year with the club. He also represented Cheshire, Denbigh, Hereford, and Shropshire. He was rector at Thurlaston from 1880 to 1908, and then Kirkby Mallory until his death in 1923.

Almost all of the players in this photograph of the Leicester Town Club, taken around 1878, represented the county at some time in their playing career. At the back: G. Bishop (umpire). From left to right, back row: F. Bassford (scorer), J. Marshall, A. Buswell, S. Newbold (umpire), J. Walker (scorer). Second row: J. Parsons, P.S. Smith, E. Holmes, E. Hill. Front row: A. Lorrimer, J. Collier, A.W. Crofts, (captain), J.A. Gill, E. Richardson.

This was the first important match to take place at the new Grace Road ground. The scorecard is not complete, the full scores being: Leicestershire 193 and 145, Australia 130 and 210-2. The Australians won by 8 wickets, and the second innings 133 by Charles Bannerman was the first century by them in England.

18

Two
Formation of the Club

CESTER COUNTY GROUND.   Photo by Broadhead &

This photograph was taken around 1890 and shows the original pavilion, with the members stand to the left, and the very rudimentary scoreboard of the time. Notice that the wickets were pitched *across* the ground, at right angles to the present square. Altogether quite a rural scene! The pavilion was erected in 1889 and survived until the present building was constructed in 1966, following the acquisition of the freehold of the ground by the club.

Above left: The present Leicestershire County Cricket Club was formed on 25 March 1879. The Sixth Earl of Lanesborough was the first president and served until 1885. *Above right:* Edward Holmes, OBE, played in some of the Leicestershire teams of the 1870s and was also secretary of the Leicestershire Cricket Association at the time. *Left:* Harry Howe JP, was a hard working member of the committee for many years.

This member's ticket for the 1879 season, in the name of T. Burdett, is in the club's archives. Thomas Burdett was a banker in Leicester, and became honorary secretary of the club in 1883, serving in that capacity until 1907. He was the Leicester representative at the meetings and discussions which led to the matches of Leicestershire and four other counties becoming first class from 1894 and 1895.

The Leicestershire team in 1879. From left to right, back row: J.H. Wheeler, A. Buswell, N.J. Hughes-Hallett, Revd G.S. Marriott, G. Chamberlain (scorer). Front row: J. Parnham, G. Panter, R.W.G. Stainton, C. Marriott (captain), W.H. Hay, W. Bottomore, F.J. Randon. Leicestershire won five of their six county matches in this, their first season.

T. Burdett. Jr.

Leicester County Cricket Club.

President: THE EARL OF LANESBOROUGH.

Vice-President: CHARLES MARRIOTT, ESQ.

Committee:

W. H. HAY, ESQ.	F. H. PAGET, ESQ.
J. D. HARRIS, ESQ.	W. B. PAGET, ESQ.
EDWIN DE LISLE, ESQ.	J. PERKINS, ESQ.
G. S. MARRIOTT, ESQ.	R. W. GILLESPIE-STAINTON, ESQ.
	REV. CANON WILLES.

Treasurer: MAJOR FREER. *Hon. Sec.:* EDWARD MILES.

MATCHES FOR THE SEASON, 1879.

June 2 and 3: Leicestershire v. Northamptonshire, at Northampton.

June   Gentlemen of Leicestershire v. Gentlemen of Staffordshire, at Leicester.

June 23, 24, and 25: Leicestershire v. Sussex, at Leicester.

July 3 and 4: Leicestershire v. Bedfordshire, at Leicester.

July   Gentlemen of Leicestershire v. Gentlemen of Staffordshire, at Lichfield.

August 6 and 7: Leicestershire v. Bedfordshire, at Luton.

August 13 and 14: Gentlemen of Leicestershire v. Uppingham Rovers, at Leicester.

August 18, 19, and 20: Leicestershire v. Northamptonshire, at Leicester.

August 28, 29, and 30: Leicestershire v. Sussex, at Brighton.

N.B. THIS TICKET IS NOT TRANSFERABLE.

Leicestershire, 1882. From left to right, back row: A.W. Crofts, G.S. Marriott, C. Marriott (captain), Lord Curzon. Middle row: T. Warren, J. Parnham, J. Wheeler, F. Turner, W. Thompson. Front row: A. Rylott, W. Bottomore. This was the team which met the Australians at Grace Road on 29 and 30 June. The Australians won a low scoring match by 74 runs – Wheeler was top scorer with 38 in the second innings! Parnham distinguished himself by taking 15 wickets for 129 runs (9 for 68 in the first innings).

John Alfred Turner was born in Leicester in 1863, the son of a local manufacturer. He was awarded a cricket blue in all four years at Cambridge, from 1883 to 1886, and also gained an athletics blue. An elegant batsman and right-arm fast bowler, Turner played for Leicestershire between 1883 and 1892, when his professional duties as a barrister permitted. His highest score in first-class cricket was 174 for Cambridge University *v.* C.I. Thornton's XI in 1886. For Leicestershire, his best was 82 not out against Surrey at The Oval in 1889. He lost an eye playing racquets at Christmas 1892, which ended his cricket career.

Charles Marriott, of Cotesbach, near Lutterworth, was a member of a well known sporting family – his father and three other brothers all excelled at various sports. He gave much support to Leicestershire cricket, being captain from 1879 to 1885, and president from 1890 to 1893 and 1903 to 1904. An Oxford blue in 1871, he surprisingly did not make many runs in first-class cricket. For Leicestershire he made just 2,331 runs between 1879 and 1893 at an average of 17.39. His only three-figure score was 148 at Lord's against the MCC in 1883.

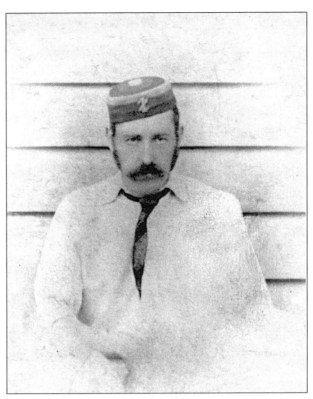

George Strickland Marriott (later the Reverend) was a younger brother of Charles, and played occasionally for Leicestershire between 1874 and 1885 without any great achievement. He also gained a blue at Oxford in 1878, but played only three matches in first-class cricket. The Revd G.S. Marriott was rector at Cotesbach from 1886 to 1897, and then of Shigglesthorne in Yorkshire until his death there in 1905. A third brother, John Marmaduke Marriott, also represented Leicestershire on occasions during the 1880s.

UPPINGHAM ROVERS v. LEICESTERSHIRE,
Wednesday and Thursday, Aug. 1 and 2.

Aylestone Road Ground.

BANK HOLIDAY, BANK HOLIDAY.

GREAT 50 MILES

→∗ BICYCLING ∗←

CHAMPIONSHIP

AT THE ABOVE GROUND, ON

.SATURDAY, AUGUST 4th, 1883.

THE BEST RIDERS IN THE WORLD WILL COMPETE

Present holder of the Cup, F. DeCIVRY, Paris.

GREAT

TEN ∴ MILES ∴ CHAMPIONSHIP

ON THE FOLLOWING

MONDAY, AUGUST 6th, 1883.

UPPINGHAM ROVERS v. LEICESTERSHIRE,
Wednesday and Thursday, Aug. 1 and 2.

HARROW WANDERERS v. LEICESTERSHIRE, Next Week ! July 23 and 24.

HARROW WANDERERS v. LEICESTERSHIRE, Next Week ! Next Week ! July 23 and 24.

Cycling was extremely popular at this time, both recreationally and as a sport, and an excellent cycle track had been laid out at the Aylestone Road Ground (Grace Road). The Fifty Miles Championship staged on August Bank Holiday Saturday 1883 followed the Leicestershire *v.* Uppingham Rovers cricket match on the previous Wednesday and Thursday. The photograph below of the event, which took place on 21 September 1887, gives a good view of the penny-farthing machines then in use, and the sporting attire (note the caps) of the time. One cannot help feeling that fifty miles in the saddle of those bicycles, before pneumatic tyres were invented, would be less than comfortable – recreation, indeed!

The match against the Australian tourists at Grace Road on 5, 6 and 7 July 1888 was described as the sensation of the season. Leicestershire were victorious by 20 runs, but it was suggested that the visitors had the worst of a poor wicket. Warren made 42 for Leicester, and the next highest score for either side was 21. 'Terror' Turner took eleven wickets for the Australians and Dick Pougher had a match analysis of 10-71 off 56 overs for Leicestershire. The county have not beaten the Australians since!

Leicestershire Cricket Ground, Aylestone Road, Leicester.

GRAND CRICKET MATCH,
AUSTRALIANS versus LEICESTERSHIRE,
THURSDAY, FRIDAY, SATURDAY, JULY 5, 6, 7. 188

LEICESTERSHIRE.

FIRST INNINGS.				SECOND INNINGS.		
WARREN, c Blackham, b Trott	..	42	l b w, b Turner	..	..	0
WHEELER, c Trott, b Turner	..	0	b Turner	..	..	11
TOMLIN, c Jarvis, b Trott	..	14	c Trott, b Turner	..		2
C. MARRIOTT, b Turner	..	5	c Worrall, b Ferris		..	12
C. E. DE TRAFFORD, c Trott, b Boyle		7	run out	..	..	1
C. C. STONE, c Blackham, b Turner		8	c Trott, b Ferris	..	..	0
POUGHER, c Worrall, b Turner	..	18	c Lyons, b Turner	..	..	11
A. W. CROFTS, b Turner	..	0	b Turner	..	..	3
J. COLLIER, not out	..	11	b Ferris	..	..	1
H. T. ARNALL-THOMPSON, b Turner	..	0	c & b Ferris	..	..	2
ATKINS, b Trott	..	9	not out	..	..	4
Extras	..	5				3
Total	..	119				50

AUSTRALIANS.

J. M. BLACKHAM, c Crofts, b A.-Thompson		2	l b w, b Pougher	..	..	3
A. C. BANNERMAN, c Crofts, b Pougher	..	2	c Crofts, b A.-Thompson	..	20
H. TROTT, c De Trafford, b A.-Thompson		0	c Wheeler, b Atkins	..	19
G. J. BONNOR, c & b Pougher	..	21	c Thompson, b Pougher	.	0
A. H. JARVIS, b A.-Thompson	..	16	c Stone, b Pougher	..	8
P. S. McDONNELL, b A.-Thompson	..	1	c A.-Thompson, b Pougher	12
C. T. B. TURNER, c Collier, b Pougher	..	8	c Stone, b A.-Thompson	..	3
J. J. LYONS, c Pougher, b A.-Thompson	..	0	c De Trafford, b Pougher	..	9
J. WORRALL, b Pougher	..	0	c and b Pougher	..	..	0
J. J. FERRIS, c Warren, b A.-Thompson	..	6	c Warren, b A.-Thompson	7
H. F. BOYLE, not out	..	6	not out	..	..	0
Extras	..					6
Total	..	62				87

Following the match engraved silver snuff-boxes were presented to the amateurs by the president, and the professionals received £5 each.

The winning Leicestershire team against the Australians in 1888. From left to right, back row: W. Atkins, A.W. Crofts, J.H. Wheeler, J. Collier. Middle row: C.C. Stone, C. Marriot, H.T. Arnall-Thompson (captain), C.E. de Trafford. Front row: T.H. Warren, A.D. Pougher, W. Tomlin.

Leicestershire in 1891. From left to right, back row: W. Tomlin, T.H. Warren, J.H. Wheeler, A. Lorrimer, A.E. Wright, A.W. Hallam. Front row: A.D. Pougher, C. Marriott, C.E. de Trafford (captain), T.S. Pearson-Gregory, J.H. Joyce.

Arthur Dick Pougher (pronounced Puffer) made his debut for the county in 1885, aged twenty, having already made a reputation in local cricket. Between then and 1893, he took over 700 wickets for Leicestershire in 'second-class' county cricket. Playing on until 1902, he scored 4,555 runs in first-class cricket, and took 535 wickets. Pougher's best bowling was 9-34 for an England XI against Surrey at The Oval in 1895. He played in one Test match for England, in South Africa during 1891/92. In Leicestershire's initial first-class match, following promotion in 1894, against Essex at Leyton, he scored a century and took 14 wickets.

Arthur Woodcock first played for Leicestershire in 1889. A right-arm fast bowler, he soon became Pougher's opening partner and they made a formidable pair! Until 1894, a coaching engagement in the USA meant that he was only available for the second half of the season. His first-class bowling record was 548 wickets at 22 runs each, with a best performance of 9-28 versus the MCC at Lord's in 1899. A tail-end batsman, he only made one fifty. He retired in 1903, but was brought back for one match as a desperate measure in 1908. Sadly, two years later, Woodcock was to take his own life with a fatal dose of poison.

William Tomlin was an attractive, fast-scoring batsman who first appeared for Leicestershire in 1887. Not his own best friend, his engagement was terminated after the 1899 season for disciplinary reasons. Billy Tomlin scored five centuries for the county, four of these in first-class matches, the highest being 140 against the MCC at Lord's in 1894. He made 2,353 runs in first-class cricket at an average of 20, entirely for Leicestershire. He died of cancer in 1910, at the early age of forty-four.

John Holland was a sound defensive batsman, whose one claim to fame was in carrying his bat through the innings for 46 out of a total of 95 versus Surrey at Grace Road in 1894. Commencing for Leicestershire in 1889, he did not make any large scores (with a best of 88 not out in 1893) and was not retained after the 1896 season. Joining the Lancashire staff in 1900, he played 12 matches between 1900 and 1902, without a great deal of success. He also appeared for Cheshire from 1910 to 1913, and died at the age of forty-five the following year.

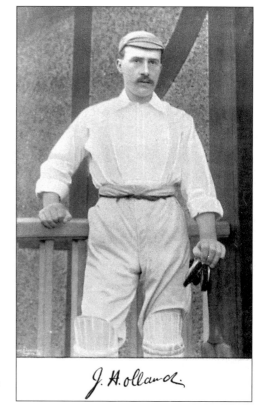

Three

First-Class Status

This view of the Aylestone Road Ground was taken in 1901, the first season it was used. The low single-storey pavilion is to the left, followed by the scoreboard, and then the members' stand. The official opening ceremony took place on Monday 13 May 1901, which was the first day of the first County Championship match of the season, Surrey being the opponents. At this time, the pavilion had not been completed, nor had all the funds to pay for the layout been realised. A 'Shilling Fund' launched by the local *Daily Post*, together with the profits from a bazaar, ensured that all was well. The ground was leased from Leicester Corporation for an initial period of twenty-one years, and was used by the club until the advent of the Second World War in 1939.

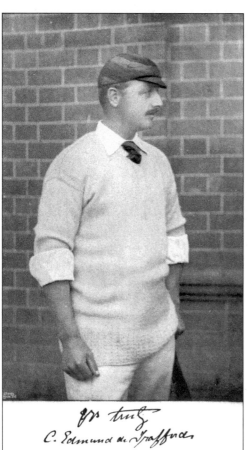

C. Edmund de Trafford

Charles Edmund de Trafford was born at Trafford Park in Manchester. Having a residence in the county, he first appeared for Leicestershire in 1888. He was a fast-footed hitter and was said to scorn the use of batting gloves! He captained the county from 1890 to 1906 and appeared on occasions afterwards until 1920 – at the age of fifty-six. In first-class cricket, de Trafford made 9,581 runs at an average of 18.67. The highest of his six centuries was 137, made against Derbyshire at Chesterfield in 1913. He was president of the County Club in 1909 and 1910.

J. P. Whiteside

John Parkinson Whiteside was born in Lancashire and represented that county from 1888 to 1890. An excellent wicketkeeper, he joined Leicestershire in 1893, playing until his retirement in 1906. He took 340 catches and made 98 stumpings in his first-class career. The regular number eleven batsman, his highest score was exactly 50. In 1903, he opened a sports outfitting shop in Aylestone Road, in partnership with Dick Pougher. Johnny Whiteside later became dressing room attendant at Aylestone Road and died in 1946 at the age of eighty-four.

Leicestershire team photograph, 1895. From left to right, back row: A. Woodcock, W. Tomlin, F.W. Stocks, J. Holland, T.H. Warren. Front row: G.W. Hillyard, A.D. Pougher, C.E. de Trafford (captain), C.C. Stone, M. Chapman. In front: J.P. Whiteside.

John Herbert King joined the Leicestershire ground staff in 1895, but did not establish himself in the team until 1899. During these early years, he also had a professional engagement with Birkenhead Park CC, where this posed photograph was taken. Despite an illustrious county career, King never made an overseas tour, and only played in one Test match for England. This was against Australia at Lord's in 1909, when he scored 60 and 4. He hit a hundred in each innings of the Players *v.* Gentlemen match in 1904. In a career lasting from 1895 to 1925, he scored 25,122 runs (average 27.33) and took 1,204 wickets (average 25.17). At the age of fifty-two, he scored 205 for Leicestershire *v.* Hampshire at Aylestone Road.

Sam Coe, from Earl Shilton, spent almost his entire lifetime with the County Club. A left-hand batsman and medium pace left-arm bowler, he played between 1896 and 1923 and was scorer from 1931 to 1949. He was made an Honorary Life Member in 1951. Coe's career batting figures were 17,438 runs for an average of 24.69, and he took 335 wickets at 32.20 each. His one double century was 252 not out for Leicestershire against Northamptonshire at Aylestone Road in 1914, which remained the highest score for the county until 1994.

Leicestershire, 1897. From left to right, back row: W. Tomlin, A. Woodcock, F. Geeson, J.H. King. Front row: C.J.B. Wood, F.W. Stocks, C.E. de Trafford (captain), A.D. Pougher, A.E. Knight. On ground: J.P. Whiteside, S. Coe.

32

The Leicestershire Cricket Ground Company, Limited.

Particulars, Plans and Conditions of Sale,

OF THE EXTREMELY VALUABLE

FULLY-LICENSED PROPERTY,

KNOWN AS THE

'Cricket Ground Hotel'

Situate on GRACE ROAD, AYLESTONE PARK, LEICESTER,

TOGETHER WITH THE HIGHLY VALUABLE AND IMPORTANT

CRICKET GROUND

ADJOINING, WITH

BICYCLE TRACK,

CONTAINING A TOTAL AREA OF

56,177 Square Yards,

OR THEREABOUTS.

H. & F. Tarratt & Sons

are instructed by the Liquidator, (Mr. R. R. Preston, Chartered Accountant,)

To Sell by Public Auction,

At the MIDLAND AUCTION MART, Market Street, Leicester,

On WEDNESDAY, 8th March, 1899,

at SEVEN o'clock in the Evening precisely, in one or two Lots as may be then determined, the above highly valuable and important Property.

Lithographed Plans and Particulars, with Conditions of Sale, may be had of Mr. R. R. PRESTON, 14, New Street; Messrs. R. J. & J. GOODACRE, Surveyors, 5, Friar Lane; The AUCTIONEERS, Market Street;

Messrs. FREER, BLUNT, ROWLATT, & WINTERTON.
OR
Solicitors, New Street;
Messrs. BURGESS & DEXTER,
Solicitors,
Berridge Street, Leicester.

The Leicestershire Cricket Ground Co. Ltd were to sell the main part of the Grace Road Ground, together with the Cricket Ground Hotel, in 1900 – the County Club using the ground until the end of that season. Presumably there was no successful bidder at this public auction? Although the sale programme states The Leicestershire Cricket Ground Company to be in liquidation, this did not actually take place until 1923.

This view of the Cricket Ground Hotel was taken around 1900. Note the proprietor, or a waiter, getting in on the act through the window! Caps and moustaches seem to be obligatory at this time.

A team photograph from 1902. From left to right, back row: H. Whitehead, F. Geeson, A.E. Knight, J.H. King. Front row: W.W. Odell, C.J.B. Wood, C.E. de Trafford (captain), R.T. Crawford, R. MacDonald. In front: J.P. Whiteside, S. Coe.

Leicestershire in 1903. From left to right, back row: H. Whitehead, T. Marlow, A.E. Knight, J.H. King. Front row: W.W. Odell, C.J.B. Wood, C.E. de Trafford (captain), R.T. Crawford, R. MacDonald. In front: J.P. Whiteside, S. Coe.

Leicestershire in 1905. From left to right, back row: G.C. Gill, A.E. Davis, H. Whitehead, A.E. Knight, T. Jayes. Front row: C.J.B. Wood, R.T. Crawford, C.E. de Trafford (captain), V.F.S. Crawford, W.W. Odell. In front S. Coe.

Albert Ernest Knight's career spanned the seasons from 1895 to 1912. He was chosen for the England tour to Australia in 1903/04, where he played all of his three Test Matches, scoring 70 not out at Sydney. A sound and consistent batsman, Knight carried his bat through an innings on five occasions for Leicestershire. The highest of his 34 centuries was 229 not out against Worcestershire at Worcester in 1903. He totalled 19,357 runs in first-class cricket, and was also a brilliant fielder in the covers.

G.A. Faulkner and A.W. Nourse leaving the field after batting for the South Africans v. Leicestershire at Aylestone Road in 1907. The South Africans won this low scoring match by 98 runs.

The Leicestershire team photograph, with officials, of 1910. Note the running fox emblem incorporated at top centre.

Cecil John Burditt Wood – usually known as 'CJB' – was reputed to be one of the most difficult batsmen to get out in county cricket. He carried his bat through an entire innings no less than seventeen times, including *both* innings of the match against the powerful bowling of Yorkshire at Bradford in 1911. Wood commenced as a professional, but after accepting the post of assistant treasurer of the County Club, reverted to amateur status. He captained Leicestershire in 1914, 1919 and 1920. In all his first-class matches he scored 23,879 runs (average 31.05) with a top score of 225.

John Shields was a fine wicketkeeper and tail-end batsman, who captained Leicestershire between 1911 and 1913. He was selected for the Gentlemen at both Lord's and The Oval in 1909, making four stumpings in the Lord's match. Shields took 170 catches and made 60 stumpings in his career, effectively between 1906 and 1913, although he returned in an emergency for one game in 1914 and again in 1923.

Held at the Grand Hotel, Leicester, on 29 November 1911, a presentation was made to C.J.B. Wood and J.H. King to honour a particular feat by each player during the previous season. Wood's was in recognition of him carrying his bat through each innings of the Yorkshire match at Bradford, and King's performance took place during the return Yorkshire match at Aylestone Road: in Yorkshire's second innings he took 7 wickets in 20 deliveries without conceding a run.

F.C. (later Sir Frederick) Toone was secretary of Leicestershire County Cricket Club from 1898 to 1902, moving on to Yorkshire in the same capacity until his retirement in 1930. During his short period with Leicester, the membership was increased from 500 to 1,800, and he was equally successful with Yorkshire. F.C. Toone was manager of the first three English touring teams to Australia after the First World War, those of 1920/21, 1924/25, and 1928/29. Following the latter tour, he was knighted for his services to the game.

Sydney Charles Packer was appointed secretary in 1910, retiring after the 1932 season; he was also honorary secretary of the Leicestershire Rugby Union for fourteen years. He was the inventor of the modern wicket covers, for which he took out patents in 1925, and they were first in use during the following season. Sydney Packer died on 29 January 1961 at the age of eighty-seven.

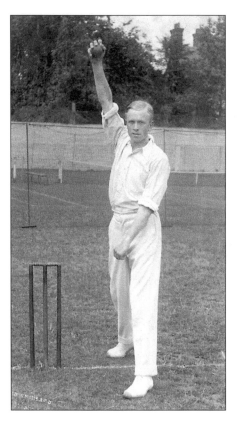

The youthful W.E. Astill in posed bowling action. Ewart Astill and George Geary became a formidable bowling partnership for Leicestershire, in fact, as all-rounders they virtually carried the county side through the 1920s. Between 1906 and 1939, Astill hit 22,731 runs, took 2.431 wickets, and made 464 catches in all first-class competition. He achieved the double in nine seasons. Despite all this, Astill only played in nine Test matches for England, all in South Africa and the West Indies.

George Geary was the other half of the partnership, and was the eldest of a family of sixteen from Barwell. He played for Leicestershire from 1912 until 1938, scoring 13,504 runs, together with 2,063 wickets and 451 catches. Geary played in 14 Tests for England. He briefly held the record for the best bowling analysis in first-class cricket, taking 10-18 against Glamorgan at Pontypridd in 1929. This was beaten three years later by Hedley Verity's 10-10. After his retirement in 1938, Geary became cricket coach at Charterhouse for twenty-one years, followed by another eleven years in the same position at Rugby School.

The first county match at the Ashby Road Ground, Hinckley, commencing on 19 August 1911. This photograph shows the opponents, Warwickshire, taking the field. Unfortunately for Leicestershire, Warwickshire won in two days by an innings and 54 runs. Despite this, the experiment was a success, 9,000 people being present over the two days. In 1936, George Geary took 13-43 against Warwickshire in an exciting match which Leicestershire won by one wicket; it was also the occasion of his second benefit. The ground was used by Leicestershire until 1937, and is now completely built over.

This view is of the Bath Grounds, Ashby-de-la-Zouch, during the first county match played there from 20 to 22 June, 1912. Derbyshire were the opponents (because of the location they were regular visitors). The last county match was played on this ground in 1964. The young Leslie Berry scored 207 here in 1928 whilst George Geary took 9 Lancashire wickets for 33 runs (14 for 98 in the match) in 1926.

Leicestershire only played two matches, one in 1913 and one in 1914, at the Fox and Goose ground at Coalville. Both games were against Worcestershire and both were won. George Geary acquired 22 wickets for 229 runs in these matches and John King scored 227 not out in 1914. The ground was opposite the Fox and Goose Hotel, at the corner of London Road and Forest Road. Forest Road Garage now occupies the frontage, while the rest of the old ground is now the Scotlands Playing Fields.

This photograph was taken at Shillinglee Park, Sussex, during a match between H.H. The Jam Sahib of Nawanagar's XII and London County XII in May 1908. From left to right: K.S. Harisinhji, W.G. Grace, C.E. de Trafford, L.S. Wells. London County were no longer playing first-class matches by this time.

William Shipman played as a right-arm fast bowler from 1908 to 1921. He was fifteen years older than his better known brother, Alan Wilfred, also a Leicestershire player. His best bowling was 9 for 83 against Surrey at The Oval in 1911 – the only season in which he exceeded a hundred wickets.

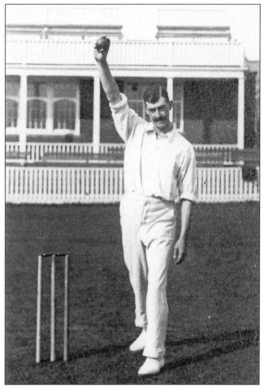

Alec Skelding was one of the game's characters, as well as being a useful right-arm fast bowler. He was thought to be one of the fastest bowlers on the county circuit during his time. Seen here in his younger days, he was a stalwart for Leicestershire from 1912 to 1929. His best season was in 1927, when he took 102 wickets at 20.80 each. He became a first-class umpire in 1931, not retiring until 1958, at the age of seventy-two.

43

The Leicestershire team in 1913. From left to right, back row: S.C. Packer (secretary), unknown, A. Lord, F. Osborn, A. Mounteney Jnr, A. Skelding, G. Geary. Middle row: C.J.B. Wood, W. Shipman, J. Shields (captain), J.H. King, W.E. Astill. Front row: W.N. Riley, H. Whitehead, W. Brown.

John Stafford Curtis played in 36 matches for the county between 1906 and 1921, his one full season being 1919; had he played regular first-class cricket, he had the ability to have made a name for himself. However, he preferred League cricket, and spent most of his playing career in Lancashire. His best performance for Leicestershire was 7 for 75 at Trent Bridge, against Nottinghamshire, in 1919.

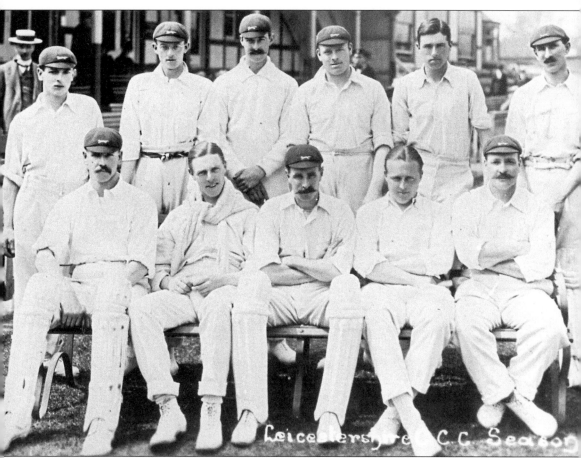

Leicestershire, 1914. From left to right, back row: T.E. Sidwell, A. Skelding, W. Shipman, A. Mounteney (junior), G. Geary, H. Whitehead. Front row: J.H. King, A.T. Sharp, C.J.B. Wood (captain), unknown, S. Coe.

William Ewart Astill in uniform during the First World War, when he obtained a commission in the Machine Gun Corps. Still serving abroad in 1919, he only returned and was demobbed in time to play in the last two matches of the season, from when he never looked back.

There was no first class cricket played in the four First World War seasons, from 1915 to 1918. The pavilion at the Aylestone Road Ground became the headquarters of the 53rd ASC Remount Depot, and the ground itself was used for drill by the Leicestershire Volunteer Regiment. Many other cricket grounds were utilised for similar wartime purposes.

Four
Inter-War Years

LEICS. v AUSTRALIANS.
1921.

The car park at the Aylestone Road Ground during the match against the Australian Touring Team in 1921. The car owning society seems to have already reached Leicester! Enthusiasts will no doubt enjoy spotting the makes and models.

Leicestershire in 1920. This photograph was taken during the match at Ashby-de-la-Zouch, and marked the final appearance of C.E. de Trafford. From left to right, back row: S. Taylor (scorer), A. Mounteney Jnr, G. Shingler, W.E. Astill, A. Skelding, H. Whitehead, W.E. Benskin, S.C. Packer (secretary). Front row: S. Coe, C.E. de Trafford, C.J.B. Wood (captain), J.H. King, T.E. Sidwell.

Albert Lord, whose real name was Albert Callington, used this alias throughout his career. The story has it that, on joining the staff and finding colleagues named King and Knight, Callington decided that he too would join the aristocracy! He played from 1910 to 1926, scoring 3,864 runs at an average of 17.32. His only three-figure score came in his final season, when he made 102 against Warwickshire at the Bulls Head Ground in Coventry.

Aubrey Temple Sharp made his debut for Leicestershire in 1908 whilst still at Repton School. His maiden century was a monumental 216 against Derbyshire at Chesterfield in 1911, but otherwise he achieved little until after the First World War. He captained the county successfully in 1921, but was not able to play regularly afterwards due to his responsibilities as a practising solicitor in Leicester. His final appearances were in 1935. Aubrey Sharp scored 5,263 runs at an average of 25.67.

Horace Charles Snary was born at Whissendine in Rutland, and was an extremely accurate medium-slow bowler – some 36 per cent of his total overs bowled were maidens! He played from 1921 to 1933, taking 419 wickets for 24.27 runs each. A stubborn, but not particularly accomplished batsman, Snary's other claim to fame came when he carried his bat through the innings for 124 not out in the match against the Indian tourists at Aylestone Road in 1932.

The Leicestershire team taking the field, led by Aubrey Sharp, on the first day of the match against the Australians in 1921. The Aylestone Road pavilion is in the background.

Aubrey Sharp and Warwick Armstrong, the Australian captain, tossing before the match. Note the size of the twenty stone Armstrong – he was known as 'The Big Ship'! The Australians won the match by an innings and 152 runs in two days. Their score of 430 for 7 declared was made from only 82.3 overs. Ted Mc Donald took 8/41 in Leicestershire's first innings and 12 wickets in the match. The attendance on the first day was 12,000 and the gate takings were £1,053 – a record for a single day at Aylestone Road.

Ewart Astill (at the table) was also an extremely accomplished billiards player. Does anyone know the identity of his opponent in the photograph, and also where and when it was taken? An urbane and outgoing personality, Astill also sang to his own piano accompaniment.

Leicestershire CCC, 1924 . From left to right, back row: F. Bale, L.G. Berry, W. Berridge, A.W. Shipman, A. Skelding, G. Geary. Front row: T.E. Sidwell, J.H. King, G.H.S. Fowke (captain), W.E. Astill, S.S. Coulson.

This lunch menu for the Leicestershire *v.* Warwickshire match at The Butts Ground, Coventry, in 1925, is a good illustration of the prices of the time. The variety of the food compares well with the fast food (only) usually available at grounds nowadays. A total of 1,017 runs were scored for the loss of 25 wickets in the match, which was drawn. Although *Wisden* states that 'a good wicket had been prepared and batsmen met with such pronounced success that a draw was inevitable.' It may be that their cause was perhaps aided by over-indulgence from the bowlers at the lunch table!

Major Gustavus Henry Spencer Fowke captained Leicestershire from 1922 to 1927. He made his debut in 1899 aged nineteen, but became a professional soldier and consequently was only able to play in eight matches before 1922. He was a prisoner of war in both the Boer War and the First World War. His first class record was 4,438 runs at an average of 18.97. Serving for some years in India with the Gordon Highlanders, Fowke hit the huge score of 309 for his Regiment against the Queen's Regiment at Peshawar in 1905.

Leicestershire CCC, 1926. From left to right, back row: F. Bale, A. Lord, A.W. Shipman, L.G. Berry, C.A.R. Coleman, S.C. Packer (secretary), T.E. Sidwell. Front row: H.A. Smith, W.E. Astill, G.B.F. Rudd (captain), G. Geary, S.S. Coulson.

Thomas Edgar Sidwell made his debut behind the stumps in 1913, playing in four matches. The regular 'keeper from 1914 until 1931, he missed only six Leicestershire matches during this period. He was called back in an emergency in 1933, when Paddy Corrall was injured. Quiet and neat in his manner, Tommy Sidwell took 583 catches and made 137 stumpings in his career. His best season with the bat was in 1928, when he scored 1,153 runs and hit two of his three centuries. He totalled 7,929 runs in first-class cricket, at an average of 15.31.

Ewart Astill and Percy Holmes of Yorkshire (left) photographed after their partnership of 330 for the fifth wicket, playing for the MCC XI against Jamaica at Sabina Park, Kingston, in March 1926. The party selected for this MCC tour to the West Indies was certainly not England's strongest, and although three matches were against the 'West Indies', these were not classed as Test matches. West Indian batting, however, was becoming much stronger, with the result that all bar three matches on this tour were drawn – MCC winning two and losing one. The first official Test matches against the West Indies were to take place on their next visit to England in 1928.

The first MCC tour to India, Burma (now Myanmar), and Ceylon (now Sri Lanka) took place in 1926/27 and was a long and arduous affair. The original programme was far too ambitious, and a number of the matches were reduced to two days in order to give adequate rest and travelling time. Long distances were travelled in scorching heat and strength sapping humidity, and on top of this was the sumptuous hospitality! George Geary and Ewart Astill were the Leicestershire representatives on this tour. Geary is in the centre of the back row on this photograph, and Astill is fourth from the left seated. The party returned undefeated in all thirty first-class matches.

The menu for the Christmas Day dinner at the Bengal Club has been signed by all of the tourists. The extra signature is that of R.J.O. 'Jack' Meyer of Cambridge University and Somerset, who had recently arrived in India to spend the next ten years as a cotton broker. He was also the founder and headmaster of Millfield School.

55

Leicestershire CCC, 1927. From left to right, back row: S.C. Packer (secretary), F. Bale, L.G. Berry, A.W. Shipman, J.C. Bradshaw, N.F. Armstrong, B. Tyler, S.S. Coulson. Front row: T.E. Sidwell, A. Skelding, G.H.S. Fowke (captain), W.E. Astill, G. Geary.

The long and the short of it! George Geary and 'Tich' Freeman, of Kent, photographed with two native girls in South Africa during the winter of 1927/28. Note the umbrellas – presumably for use as parasols. Both Geary and Astill, together with Eddie Dawson, took part in this MCC tour.

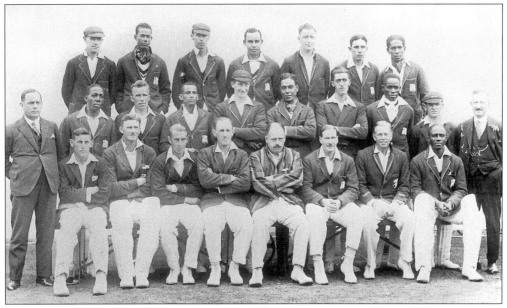

Leicestershire *v*. West Indians at Aylestone Road in 1928. The Leicester players are, from left to right, back row: N.F. Armstrong, A.W. Shipman, L.G. Berry. Middle row: H.C. Snary, H.A. Smith, C.A.R. Coleman, T.E. Sidwell. Front row: J.C. Bradshaw, G.B.F. Rudd (captain), W.E. Astill. H. Riley is absent from the photograph.

This display in Burton's store window was to advertise the Membership Campaign of 1928. The object was to recruit 1,000 new members to fund the replacement of the old enclosure stand at Aylestone Road, which was severely damaged by fire in July. A more substantial structure was built during the winter, and was ready for use in the following season.

Five captains of Leicestershire – E.W. Dawson, Sir Arthur (later Lord) Hazlerigg, C.J.B. Wood, G.H.S. Fowke and G.B.F. Rudd. The photograph was taken on 14 September 1928, at a match between E.W. Dawson's XI and J.W. Dixie-Smith's XI in celebration of the County Club's fifty year Jubilee.

Only two county matches were played at the College Ground in Loughborough. The first was in 1928, against Derbyshire. This photograph is of play in progress during the second match, the following year, when the opponents were Glamorgan. Leicestershire won this match by an innings and 9 runs. Glamorgan's second innings total of 98 occupied 81 overs, 40 of which were maidens. Geary and Astill each took 10 wickets in the match. The ground is now covered by the Student Union building.

Sir Arthur Grey Hazlerigg, Bart. (created first Baron Hazlerigg in 1945), captained Leicestershire in all four of his playing years, from 1907 to 1910. A tail-end batsman, with a highest score of 55 not out, he proved to be an efficient and popular captain. A well-known public figure in Leicestershire, he was Lord Lieutenant of the county. Sir Arthur supported the County Club for many years and was president in 1930, when this photograph was taken.

Arthur Grey Hazlerigg (pictured here in his playing days), succeeded as the second Baron Hazlerigg on the death of his father in 1949. He won blues at Cambridge in 1930, 1931, and 1932 and was captain in his final year – a season in which he scored all three of his first-class hundreds. He played for Leicestershire from 1930 to 1934 and captained the county in 1934. His figures in first-class cricket were 2,515 runs (average 25.92) and 112 wickets for 31.04 each. A magnificent slip fielder, he held 75 catches in 66 matches. He was awarded the Military Cross in the Second World War, during which he reached the rank of Major. Lord Hazlerigg is currently Leicestershire's oldest living former player.

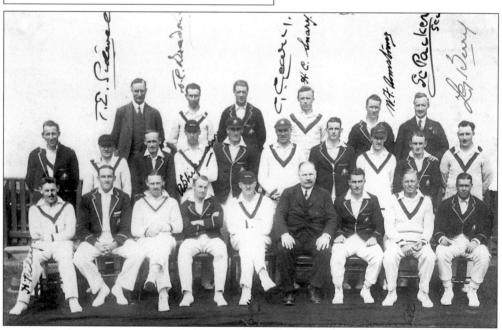

A page of Leicestershire autographs from 1930. The signatures, from the top downwards, are: J.A. de Lisle, A.G. Hazlerigg, W.E. Astill, H.C. Snary, N.F. Armstrong, H. Riley, R. Coleman, H.A. Smith, L.G. Berry, G. Geary, A. Shipman, T.E. Sidwell and J.C. Bradshaw.

Leicestershire *v.* the Australians in 1930 – although the original caption states 1936! The Leicestershire players have signed the photograph. The young Don Bradman is seated fourth from the left on the front row, followed by J.A. de Lisle, the Leicestershire captain, and Sir A.G. Hazlerigg, the club president.

W.E. Astill in action at the crease. There is no information as to when or where he is playing – does anyone recognise the ground, or the identity of the wicketkeeper?

Ewart Astill again, batting at Lord's against Middlesex on 25 August 1932: he has just hit H.W. Lee to the boundary for the third ball in succession. W.F.F. Price is the Middlesex wicketkeeper. Middlesex countered Leicestershire's first innings total of 479 for 6 declared with a score of 573 and the match was drawn.

The Leicestershire team in 1931. From left to right, back row: F.J. Bowley, H.C. Snary, N.F. Armstrong, C.A.R. Coleman, L.G. Berry, J.C. Bradshaw. Front row: T.E. Sidwell, W.E. Astill, E.W. Dawson (captain), G. Geary, A.W. Shipman.

Percy 'Paddy' Corrall made his debut at Fenner's in 1930, batting two hours for four runs. He took over from Tommy Sidwell as regular 'keeper in 1932. Paddy suffered a serious head injury during the 1933 season, which initially was thought to have finished his career. Happily he recovered to resume playing in the following season. In 1937, he lost his place in the side to George Dawkes, returning in 1946 when Dawkes went to Derbyshire, and he retired in 1951. In the immediate post-war years, Corrall stumped over 100 batsmen off the bowling of Jack Walsh. In a career of 288 matches, he caught 382 batsmen, and stumped 186.

Leslie Berry and Alan Shipman walking out to commence an innings. Leicestershire's regular opening pair during most of the time that they played together, they made 14 first-wicket partnerships of over 100. The highest of these stands was 219 against Hampshire at Portsmouth in 1935, when Berry scored 151 and Shipman 94.

The Packe family – from left to right: R.J., M. St J., E.C., Miss M.O and C.W.C. This was a talented sporting family, headed by Lt Col E.C. Packe DSO, OBE, of Great Glen Hall. E.C. played for the MCC and Leicestershire Gentlemen, and was joint honorary secretary of the County Club from 1933 to 1935. Charles William Christopher, the eldest son, played for Leicestershire between 1929 and 1934, and was killed in action in Normandy in 1944. Robert Julian only appeared on three occasions for the County, dying of dysentery in India in 1935, aged twenty-two. Michael St John played for Leicestershire between 1936 and 1939, and was captain for the last season before the Second World War. During the war, he took part in both the evacuation from Dunkirk and the airborne landings at Arnhem in 1944.

Anthony Riddington was a left-handed all-rounder who met with only moderate success from his debut in 1931 until 1934. He then left the staff and took professional engagements in Scotland up until the Second World War. Returning to Leicestershire in 1946, he showed much better form and made his only century, 104 not out at Northampton against Northamptonshire. He dropped out of the team in 1950.

Leicestershire taking the field at Aylestone Road in 1936. From left to right: H.A. Smith, N.F. Armstrong, (features obscured but probably) L.G. Berry, C.S. Dempster (captain), F.T. Prentice, A.W. Shipman. Following behind are: G. Geary and P. Corrall (obscured by Shipman).

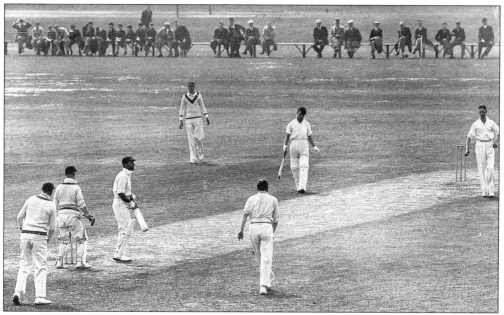

Action from the first day of the Leicestershire *v.* South Africa match at Aylestone Road in 1935. H.F. Wade, the South African captain, has just been bowled by W.H. Marlow after scoring 9 runs. Leicestershire were set 403 to win in their second innings, but were bowled out early on the third morning for 233.

General Sir John Aubrey Taylor Sharp KCB, MC, was the son of A.T. Sharp. Having attended Cambridge without getting a blue, he played four times for Leicestershire between 1937 and 1946. The Military Cross was won in August 1942 for gallant and distinguished services in the Middle East, a bar being added in August the following year. General Sharp was Commander in Chief of Allied Forces Northern Europe from 1974 until he died suddenly in Oslo on 15 January 1977 at the age of fifty-nine.

First appearing for the county in 1924, Leslie Berry soon became a pillar of their batting strength for many years. He exceeded 1,000 runs in eighteen seasons, his best being 2,446 in 1937, when he also hit seven centuries. Playing in 609 matches – all but four of them for Leicestershire – he scored 30,225 runs at an average of 30.26, with 45 hundreds. His highest score was 232 against Sussex at Aylestone Road in 1930. He was appointed county captain in 1946, and led the side for three seasons. Retiring in 1951, Les Berry was coach at Uppingham School until 1979 and he died in 1985 at the age of seventy-eight.

The teams, umpires, and officials at the first county match to be played at Oakham School Ground in August 1935. Leicestershire won this match, against Kent, by 10 wickets. Three more matches were played at Oakham School, in 1936, 1937 and 1938, Leicestershire losing all three.

Frank Prentice returning to the pavilion at Aylestone Road after hitting 163 against Hampshire on 8 May 1937. F.T. Prentice was a Yorkshireman who qualified for Leicester in 1935. A consistent right-hand bat, he made 10,997 runs – all for the county – at an average of 27.70. The highest of his 17 centuries was 191 against Nottinghamshire at Park Road, Loughborough, in 1949. His gentle off-breaks brought 117 rather expensive wickets. He played a few matches as an amateur in 1951, before retiring to concentrate on his business interests.

George Owen Dawkes was just 16 years and 328 days old when he made his first appearance for the County in 1937 and at that time was their youngest ever player. Brought in when Paddy Corrall was injured, he kept wicket so well that he retained his place to the conclusion of the 1939 season. After the Second World War he moved to Derbyshire, playing on until 1961. A competent batsman, with one century to his credit, Dawkes scored 11,411 runs in all his first-class cricket. He made 148 stumpings and took 895 catches.

Leicestershire CCC, 1938. From left to right, back row: G. Lester, L.D. Thursting, P. Cherrington, G.S. Watson, S. Coe (scorer), H.A. Smith, M. Tompkin. Middle row: G.O. Dawkes, N.F. Armstrong, G. Geary (captain), L.G. Berry, W.H. Flamson, H. Moore (masseur). In front: R.A. Adcock.

A view of the Aylestone Road Ground, taken during the match against Nottinghamshire on 1 June 1939. All seems to be peace, light, and tranquility, but the war clouds were forming over Europe. Note The Meet stand, built in 1909, which was subsequently taken to Grace Road.

Another view of The Meet, now becoming derelict during the Second World War. The Aylestone Road Ground was occupied by the National Fire Service at the beginning of the war, followed by the US Army Pioneer Corps, who remained until the winter of 1944. It was then taken over by Leicester Corporation, who required it for an extension to the adjoining electricity works.

George Sutton Watson had played a few games for Kent as an amateur, before commencing a professional career with Leicestershire in 1934. A forcing right-hand bat and splendid fieldsman, he scored 8,566 runs (average 22.97) before retiring after the 1950 season. Watson was also an amateur international footballer in his youth, before becoming professional with Charlton Athletic, Crystal Palace, and Clapton Orient.

No. 4 Platoon, 'A' Company, 2nd South Leicester Home Guard pictured in front of the Aylestone Road pavilion in 1944.

Five

Light and Darkness

An aerial photograph of the Grace Road Ground, taken in the late 1940s, well before any
refurbishment or improvement works had commenced.

Play in progress at Egerton Park, Melton Mowbray, during the Somerset match in 1946. Only three county matches were to be played at Egerton Park – the Somerset game in 1946, against Lancashire in 1947, and Kent in 1948. Leicestershire lost all three of these fixtures.

The match at Park Road, Loughborough, between Leicestershire and Nottinghamshire in 1947, which Leicestershire won by 10 wickets. David Gower was to play his first club cricket for Loughborough Town on this ground.

Gerry Lester initially played as a leg-break bowler in 1937, but after the war his batting developed, and he became a useful all-rounder. In all, he took part in 373 matches for Leicestershire, scoring 12,857 runs (average 21.61) and taking 307 wickets for 35.45 each. He was appointed coach on his retirement from playing in 1958, and held the post until 1966.

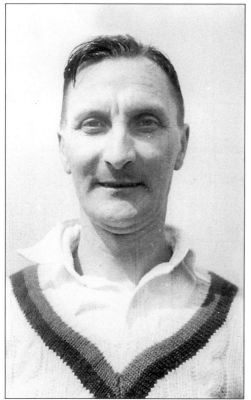

James Sperry was a left-arm fast-medium bowler, whose career also spanned the Second World War. He was to take 492 wickets between 1937 and 1952. His best performance was 7 for 19 against Hampshire at Aylestone Road in 1939. Jim Sperry had previously been a miner and died on 21 April 1997 at the age of eighty-seven.

The Leicestershire team in 1948. From left to right, back row: G. Lester, M. Tompkin, W.B. Cornock, S. Coe (scorer), A. Riddington, V.E. Jackson, J.H. Howard. Front row: J.E. Walsh, J. Sperry, L.G. Berry (captain), P. Corrall, G.S. Watson.

Leicestershire pays its last tribute to Haydon Smith, before the Worcestershire match at Grace Road on 10 August 1948. From 1925 to 1939, he took 1,076 wickets for 25.99 runs each, with a best of 8-40 v. Gloucestershire at Bristol in 1948. He died suddenly from heart failure at the early age of forty-seven.

John Edward Walsh, born in Sydney, New South Wales, was employed by Sir Julien Cahn, and played a few first-class matches for his team. He also played for Leicestershire as an amateur until the outbreak of the Second World War. Becoming a professional in 1946, by the time he finished in 1957, his slow left-arm spin had accounted for 1,190 victims, having taken ten or more wickets in a match no less than 26 times. His best bowling was 9 for 101 for Sir J. Cahn's XI *v.* Glamorgan in 1938. Also an attacking batsman, Jack Walsh completed the 'double' in 1952.

Four Leicestershire captains, taken at Market Harborough in 1949. From left to right: S.J. Symington (1949), C.J.B. Wood (1914, 1919, 1920), C.E. de Trafford (1890-1906) and L.G. Berry (1946-1948).

Leicestershire CCC, 1951. From left to right, back row: G.A. Smithson, M.A.J. Sargent, P.F. Saunders, C.T. Spencer, T.J. Goodwin, J. Firth, V.S. Munden. Front row: J.E. Walsh, V.E. Jackson, C.H. Palmer (captain), G. Lester, M. Tompkin.

Maurice Tompkin coming in after scoring 107 not out against Middlesex at Grace Road on 27 May 1952. This was his second century of the match, having made 156 in the first innings. Leicestershire won by 7 wickets. Sadly, he was to die following an operation four years later, aged only thirty-seven.

A group of players at the indoor nets at Grace Road in 1953. In the photograph are: J.S. Savage, V.S. Munden, W.H. Ashdown (coach), J. Sperry, M.F. Hickman, F. Parker, P.T. Smith, M. Tompkin, M.R. Hallam, R. Julian, B.S. Boshier. W.H. Ashdown is the old Kent player, who was coach at Leicestershire from 1951 to 1961 and scorer from 1966 to 1969.

Charles Terence Spencer was awarded his county cap in his first season, 1952, and between then and 1974 took 1,367 wickets at an average of 26.69 with his right-arm, medium-pace bowling. He was given a Test trial in 1953, and was unlucky not to get any national honours. A hard hitting tail-ender with a highest score of 90, his best bowling performance was 9 for 63 against Yorkshire at Huddersfield in 1954. Terry Spencer is a nephew of Haydon Smith and was a first-class umpire from 1979 to 1983.

The present concrete terracing and seating on the popular side at Grace Road was built during the winter of 1952/53. The old enclosure stand from Aylestone Road, now The Meet, was at the same time dismantled and re-erected, with improvements, adjacent to the new terracing.

The refreshment bar at the Milligan Road end of the ground, during the 1950s. This is now the groundsmen's hut.

A signed photograph of Charles Palmer holding the ball with which he took an astonishing 8 for 7 against Surrey at Grace Road in 1955. After twelve overs he had taken all of those wickets without conceding a run, all of the runs off his bowling coming in the last two overs. Seven of his victims were clean bowled. The match scores were Leicestershire 114 and 165, Surrey 77 and 203-3 – the mighty Surrey eventually winning by 7 wickets despite Palmer's remarkable performance.

Gerald Arthur Smithson was specially registered from Yorkshire in 1951, having already played for England. A 'Bevin Boy' in 1947, he was selected for the MCC tour to the West Indies the following winter, and had to be given Government permission to take part. He played for Leicestershire until 1956, scoring 5,305 runs for the county at 22.10.

Leicestershire, 1955. From left to right, back row: F.N. Bloxom (scorer), J. Firth, E.F. Phillips, T.J. Goodwin, C.T. Spencer, M.J.K. Smith, R.A. Diment, V.S. Munden. Front row: J.E. Walsh, M. Tompkin, C.H. Palmer (captain), G. Lester, V.E. Jackson.

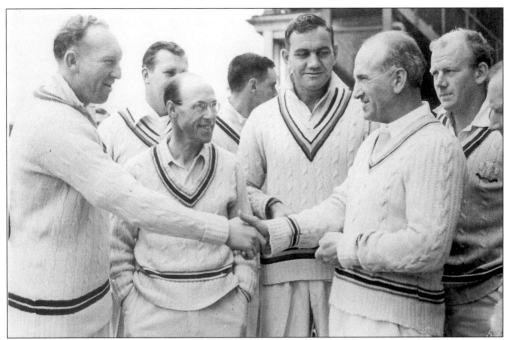

Jack Walsh chose the previously mentioned Surrey game in 1955 as his benefit match. He is shown here receiving the good wishes of the Surrey captain, Stuart Surridge, together with (from left to right) Jim Laker, Charles Palmer, Peter May (partly obscured), Alec Bedser and Tony Lock.

Vic Jackson surveys the dismal prospects for his benefit match. The first day of the Hampshire match at Grace Road in 1956 was washed out by rain, and play did not begin until after lunch on the second day. When Hampshire batted he took the first four wickets to fall and in the Leicester innings he was top scorer with 41. Jackson left county cricket at the end of the season and was professional for Rawtenstall in the Lancashire League during 1957 and 1958. He later returned to Australia, where he was killed in a car accident on 28 January 1965, aged forty-eight.

Leicestershire 2nd XI in 1952. From left to right, back row: M.F. Turner, J.S. Savage, P.F. Saunders, R.C. Smith, F.G. Foulds, D. Goodson, R. Wheelet, ? Vann, P.T. Smith. Front row: H. Moore, (masseur), J. Sperry, W.H. Ashdown (coach), J.M. Josephs (captain), M.R. Hallam, M.A.J. Sargeant, S. Berridge (scorer).

John Scholes Savage, a Lancastrian off-break bowler, joined Leicestershire in 1953. After leaving the county in 1966, he returned to Lancashire to play a few matches between 1967 and 1969, subsequently coaching them for a number of years. He captured 965 wickets for 24.64 runs each, and took 100 wickets in a season three times.

Maurice Hallam took 182 innings to register his initial first-class century, but thereafter quickly developed into a most consistent opening batsman and was unlucky never to be chosen for England. He exceeded 1,000 runs in a season thirteen times – three times reaching 2,000 – and scored 32 centuries, between 1950 and 1970. He was captain of Leicestershire from 1963 to 1965, and again in 1968. Of his four double centuries, the highest was 210 not out against Glamorgan at Grace Road in 1959, also making 157 in the second innings of the same match. His career record was 24,488 runs at an average of 28.84. A brilliant slip fielder, he took 453 catches in 504 matches. Maurice coached at Uppingham after retiring and he died in Leicester on 1 January 2000.

Raymond Julian was the county's regular wicketkeeper between 1959 and 1965, having previously understudied Jack Firth since 1953, at the age of sixteen. He took 382 catches and made 39 stumpings in his career. He captained the Second XI from 1968 to 1971. Ray Julian was appointed to the first-class umpires list in 1972 and is still giving decisions in his quiet and unobtrusive manner.

The team in 1958. From left to right, back row: R. Julian, J. van Geloven, B.S. Boshier, T.J. Goodwin, J.S. Savage, G.W. Burch. Front row: C.T. Spencer, M.R. Hallam, W. Watson (captain), R.A. Diment, A.C. Revill.

Jack van Geloven was specially registered from Yorkshire in 1956, having played three matches for them in the previous season. A useful all-rounder, he did the 'double' for Leicestershire in 1962. Playing until 1965, his career record was 7,522 runs at an average of 19.43 and 486 wickets at 28.62. The highest of his five hundreds was 157 not out against Somerset at Grace Road in 1960. He was a first-class umpire from 1977 to 1983.

Willie Watson was another Yorkshire recruit in 1958, and was county captain until 1961. In the twilight of a distinguished career, which had commenced with Yorkshire in 1939, he brought stability to the Leicestershire batting. His record for Leicestershire from 1958 to 1964 was 7,728 runs (average 42.46), including 18 centuries, with a top score of 217 not out. A double international, Watson played 23 Test matches for England and gained four soccer caps. He was also a Test selector from 1962 to 1964.

Harold Dennis Bird MBE, in his younger days. 'Dickie' Bird had played a few matches for Yorkshire before joining Leicestershire in 1960. He had a good first season, scoring 1,028 runs, and hitting one century. However, he struggled thereafter and faded from the side in 1964. Following some years coaching and playing as a club professional in the West Country, he was appointed to the first-class umpires list in 1970. This was his true metier and Dickie was put on the Test match panel in 1973, commencing the distinguished second career for which he has achieved worldwide renown. He finally retired in 1998, having umpired in 66 Test matches (the record) and 69 one-day internationals.

Action from the Middlesex *v.* Leicestershire match at Lord's on 17 July 1962. Stanley Jayasinghe (Leicestershire) has just driven A.E. Moss for four. Middlesex won this close fought game by 25 runs.

More action at Lord's from another Middlesex *v.* Leicestershire match, this time from July 1964. This photograph was taken on the final day as Jack Birkenshaw of Leicester is caught by the Middlesex wicketkeeper, John Murray, off the bowling of Freddie Titmus, for 9. Middlesex were to win again, this time by 130 runs.

Stanley Jayasinghe, from Ceylon, was a forcing right-hand batsman who played in the Lancashire League before qualifying for Leicestershire in 1962. Unfortunately, he decided to return to his native country after the 1965 season. Making over 1,000 runs in all four seasons with the county, his total record for Leicestershire was 5,223 runs at an average of 27.78

Leicestershire in 1965. From left to right, back row: G.F. Cross, J. Birkenshaw, R.J. Barratt, S. Jayasinghe, B.J. Booth, P.T. Marner, J. Cotton. Front row: C.T. Spencer, J.S. Savage, M.R. Hallam (captain), C.C. Inman, R. Julian.

Fund-raising on a large scale was necessary to finance the many improvements which were undertaken at Grace Road during the mid-1960s. This Leicester City Transport bus is carrying an advertising panel for the Leicestershire County Cricket Club lottery – such ventures were just becoming very popular.

Alec Skelding and Paddy Corrall photographed in their umpire's coats, when they were officiating together sometime during the 1950s. Skelding was on the first-class umpires list from 1931 to 1958, standing in 457 County Championship matches during this time. Corrall officiated from 1952 to 1958 and umpired in 122 Championship matches.

H.J. 'Walter' White, seen here sitting on the gang mower, was head groundsman at Aylestone Road from 1935 to 1939 and at Grace Road from 1946 to 1949, returning in 1958. He retired in October 1973.

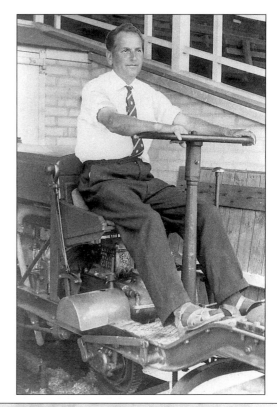

A match in progress at Snibston Colliery Ground, Coalville. Leicestershire played on this ground seven times between 1957 and 1966, after which the club's policy changed regarding out matches. Just at that time the North Leicestershire Miners' Welfare Community Centre was opened at the ground, and many improvements were carried out. One further county match was played here in 1982, and one John Player League match in 1970.

Two young Leicestershire Second XI players photographed in 1965. Roger Tolchard, on the right, was just on the brink of a long and successful career with the county, as both batsman and wicketkeeper. The other youngster, Riaz (Ray) Rehman was only to play one first-class match in 1966, whilst qualifying for the county; a promising cricket career was ended tragically when he was killed in a road accident in July 1966 whilst travelling to a Second XI match.

Michael Turner at his desk in 1966. A lifetime career with Leicestershire County Cricket Club commenced in 1951, when he joined the ground staff. Failing to make the grade as a player, he was appointed cashier in 1958, and subsequently assistant secretary. In August of 1961 he was appointed secretary, became secretary-manager in 1970 and chief executive in 1988. He retired in 1993. During this time, Mike Turner was responsible for implementing and overseeing all of the many developments at Grace Road, both on and off the field. He has left a rich legacy.

Six

Success at Last

Roger Tolchard (left) and Paul Haywood hold aloft the Benson & Hedges Cup at Lord's on 22 July 1972. Leicestershire had beaten Yorkshire by 5 wickets in the inaugural Benson & Hedges competition. Chris Balderstone won the Gold Award for his innings of 41 not out. The county featured in three of the first four finals: they lost to Surrey in 1974 and were the winners again in 1975.

The opening of the new pavilion at Grace Road on 25 June 1966 by the Lord Bishop of Leicester, the Rt Revd R.R. Williams DD. Next to the Bishop is William Bentley MBE, the president, and then Mike Turner. Members of the Leicestershire and Surrey teams are also in the photograph. The structure was built on the site of the old pavilion, which had stood since 1889.

A group on the top of the new pavilion. From left to right: M.St J. Packe, C.H. Palmer, E.W. Dawson, E.E. Snow, A.T. Sharp, Lord Hazlerigg and L.G. Berry. All except Eric Snow were former captains of Leicestershire.

Team photograph, 1966. From left to right, back row: W.H. Ashdown (scorer), P.T. Marner, R.W. Tolchard, J. Cotton, G.F. Cross, J. Birkenshaw, B.J. Booth, M.E.J.C. Norman. Front row: C.C. Inman, M.R. Hallam, G.A.R. Lock (captain), C.T. Spencer, J.S. Savage.

Roger Tolchard captured in mid-appeal! As there is no sign of the ball in his gloves, presumably he is asking for an lbw decision. Tolchard kept wicket for Leicestershire between 1965 and 1983, captaining the county in his final three seasons. He is the holder of the Leicestershire record for wicketkeeping dismissals (794 catches, 109 stumpings) and his right-handed batting also brought him 13,895 runs for the county. Selected for the England 1976/77 tour of India as reserve 'keeper, he played in four of the Test matches as a batsman.

Leicestershire in 1969. From left to right, back row: B.R. Knight, P.T. Marner, R.W. Tolchard, B.J. Booth, R.J. Barratt, J. Birkenshaw, B. Dudleston. Front row: C.T. Spencer, G.D. McKenzie, R. Illingworth (captain), M.R. Hallam, C.C. Inman.

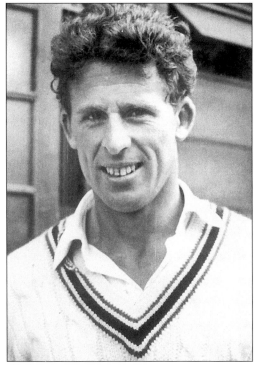

Brian Joseph Booth, a right-hand bat and leg-break bowler, started his career playing for Lancashire in 1956. He joined Leicestershire in 1964 and left after the 1973 season to play league cricket. He scored 15,298 runs in first-class cricket (average 27.91), and took 146 wickets at 32.03. The best of his 18 centuries was 183 not out for Lancashire *v.* Oxford University at Old Trafford in 1961.

Clive Clay Inman had appeared for his native Ceylon and was professional at Penzance whilst qualifying for Leicestershire. An attractive, hard hitting left-hander, it was a great pity that he retired early. For Leicestershire, between 1961 and 1971, he made 12,364 runs at an average of 34.54, exceeding 1,000 runs in eight of those seasons. Against Nottinghamshire at Trent Bridge in 1965 he scored 51 in eight minutes, hitting 5 sixes and 5 fours. Whilst this is a world record, it must be remembered that it was made in contrived circumstances, against declaration bowling.

Ken Higgs came to Leicestershire in 1972 after an extremely successful career with Lancashire, during which he had played in fifteen Tests for England. His second career ended in 1979, in which season he captained the county. The Leicestershire coach from 1981 to 1990, he made six more emergency appearances, the last being in 1986. His right-arm accurate medium-pace bowling earned 1,536 wickets at an average of 23.61 runs each in first-class cricket. Another claim to fame was a partnership of 228, with Ray Illingworth, for the tenth wicket for Leicestershire v. Northamptonshire at Grace Road in 1977 – the county's highest score for the last wicket.

Brian Fettes Davison, an aggressive batsman from Rhodesia, qualified for Leicestershire in 1970 and played until 1983, having being captain in 1980. He continued to play in Rhodesia and then in Tasmania, to which he eventually emigrated, until 1987/88. He also had a single season with Gloucestershire in 1985. In all his first-class cricket he scored 27,453 runs (average 39.96) and made 53 hundreds. A brilliant fieldsman, he took 338 catches. Brian Davison followed a political career in Tasmania for many years and now runs an antiques business in Launceston.

John Christopher Balderstone was another import from Yorkshire. Having no success with his native county, he signed for Leicestershire in 1971. His right-hand batting improved so much that he gained two caps for England v. West Indies in 1976. Retiring in 1986, his total figures were 19,034 runs at an average of 34.11 and 310 wickets at 26.32. He became a first-class umpire in 1988 and was still on the list when he died of cancer on 6 March 2000. Chris Balderstone was also a professional footballer and, during September 1975, he played cricket for Leicestershire at Chesterfield against Derbyshire in the day and in the evening appeared for Doncaster Rovers in a Division Four match against Brentford.

Paddy Clift, on his debut for the county in 1975, batting against the Australians at Grace Road. The Australian wicketkeeper in the photograph is Rodney Marsh. Paddy was recommended to Leicestershire by fellow Rhodesian Brian Davison. A dependable all-rounder, by the time he finished playing in 1987, he had scored over 5,000 runs and taken over 500 wickets for Leicestershire. A popular personality, his sudden death from cancer at the age of forty-three on 2 September 1996 was a great shock to all who knew him.

Graham McKenzie bowls Barry Richards with the sixth ball of the match in the Benson & Hedges Cup semi-final against Hampshire at Grace Road on 2 July 1975. The non-striker is Gordon

Greenidge, who went on to score 111. Roger Tolchard is the Leicester wicketkeeper and the two slips are Ken Higgs and John Steele. David Evans, the ex-Glamorgan player, is the umpire.

The Leicestershire team in celebratory mood at Lord's! From left to right: Roger Tolchard, Geoff Cross, Ray Illingworth, Chris Balderstone, Barry Dudleston, Ken Higgs, Peter Booth (behind Higgs), Jeff Tolchard (twelfth man), Norman McVicker (obscured), John Steele and Brian Davison (who has already changed). Graham McKenzie is not in the photograph.

The same silverware, but this time held by Mike Turner (left) and Ray Illingworth.

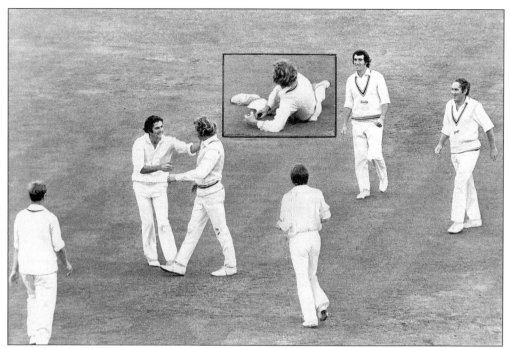

Still with the 1975 Benson & Hedges Cup final – the Leicestershire players congratulate Brian Davison after brilliantly catching Mike Brearley, the Middlesex skipper. First to him is Norman McVicker, the bowler. The other players are, from left to right: Ken Higgs, Barry Dudleston, John Steele, and Ray Illingworth. The inset shows how it was done.

Leicestershire staff and officials in 1975. At the centre of the front row are Charles Palmer (honorary secretary), Ray Illingworth (captain), William Bentley (president), Ken Higgs (vice-captain) and Mike Turner (secretary-manager). A youthful David Gower is fifth from the left in the back row.

101

Ray Illingworth batting and bowling. Already with an international reputation, he arrived to captain Leicestershire from 1969 to 1978, and led the county through the most successful decade in their history, including their first ever County Championship in 1975. He won 31 of his 61 Test caps whilst with Leicestershire.

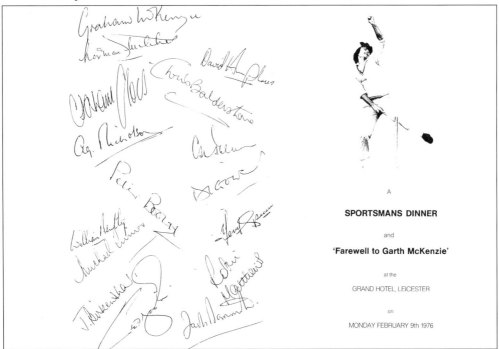

A

SPORTSMANS DINNER

and

'Farewell to Garth McKenzie'

at the

GRAND HOTEL, LEICESTER

on

MONDAY FEBRUARY 9th 1976

A menu cover, autographed by Leicestershire players and others, from the 'Farewell to Garth McKenzie' dinner at the Grand Hotel, Leicester, in February 1976. Spot the odd ones out.

Barry Dudleston batting during the Leicestershire *v.* West Indies match at Grace Road in 1976. There were five centuries (and a 98) in this match of nearly 1,200 runs – which included three declarations. The West Indies eventually won by 7 wickets. Dudleston scored 24 and 13.

The Leicestershire squad in 1979. Ken Higgs, the captain, is in the centre of the front row, flanked by William Bentley and Mike Turner. Note the hirsute appearance of most of the players, in keeping with the fashion of the time.

Andy Roberts, the West Indian fast bowler, was signed as an overseas player in 1981, although not without some criticism. Also having a contract with Haslingden in the Lancashire League, his appearances for Leicestershire were restricted. In four seasons he was only able to play in 36 matches – but he took 141 wickets at 21.75 runs each. He managed an impressive 8 for 56 against Glamorgan at Grace Road in 1982.

Leslie Brian Taylor, a miner from Earl Shilton, first appeared in 1977, and soon made an impact with his fast-medium right-arm bowling. He took 75 wickets at 21.71 in 1981, but decided to join a rebel tour to South Africa the following winter, and was banned from Test cricket for three years. His two Test caps came in 1985 against Australia, at Edgbaston and The Oval. Les Taylor retired in 1990, having taken 581 wickets at 25.21 in his first-class career.

Action from the Leicestershire *v.* Northamptonshire match at Grace Road on 24 May 1975 as John Steele is lbw to Sarfraz Nawaz for 2 on the first morning. Barry Dudleston is the non-striker and George Sharp the Northants 'keeper. Despite a bad start, when four wickets fell for 16 runs, Leicestershire eventually won the match by the margin of 143 runs. Steele, Dudlestone and Sharp are all currently on the first-class umpires list.

The Leicestershire team for the Benson & Hedges Cup final in 1985. The photograph was taken at Grace Road. From left to right, back row: G. Blackburn (scorer), M.A. Garnham, I.P. Butcher, J.P. Agnew, L.B. Taylor, N.G.B. Cook, G.J. Parsons, J.J. Whitaker. Front row: P.B. Clift, J.C. Balderstone, D.I. Gower (captain), P. Willey, N.E. Briers.

David Gower batting against the Australians at Grace Road in 1985. W.B. Phillips is the Australian wicketkeeper. David is executing a typical left-hander's lofted on-drive.

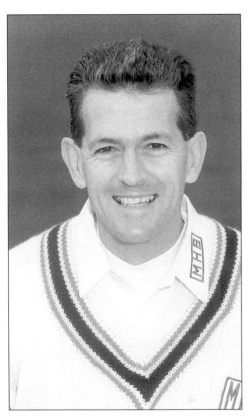

Nigel Edwin Briers made his debut for Leicestershire against Cambridge University in 1971, aged 16 years and 103 days, thus becoming the youngest ever player to represent the county. It was not until 1978, when his batting had developed, that he gained a regular place in the team, but he soon became a dependable opener. He was captain from 1990 to 1995, retiring at the end of this period. Playing only for Leicestershire, he made 18,726 runs at 33.02. The highest of his 31 hundreds was 201 not out against Warwickshire at Edgbaston in 1983.

Gordon Parsons was another player who took a while to establish himself. A right-arm medium-pace bowler and useful bat, he was not retained after the 1985 season and spent the following three years with Warwickshire. He returned to Leicestershire in 1989, retiring in 1997. He also spent several winters playing in the Currie Cup in South Africa. His total tally in first-class cricket was 6,763 runs and 809 wickets. He is the brother-in-law of Hansie Cronje, the former South African captain.

Peter Willey batting at Grace Road. In a long and varied career, he first played for Northamptonshire as a sixteen year old in 1966, won 26 Test caps for England, joined Leicestershire in 1984, was captain in 1987 and finished playing in 1991. A genuine all-rounder, during this time he made 24,361 runs at 30.56 and took 756 wickets at 30.95. Peter Willey became a first-class umpire in 1993 and was appointed to the ICC International Umpires Panel in 1996.

Jon Agnew, a right-arm fast bowler, played three Tests for England in 1984 and 1985 without success, but was strangely ignored in 1987 and 1988 when taking 101 and 93 wickets respectively. He retired at his peak in 1990 to take up a career in journalism and broadcasting. Between 1978 and 1990, he took 666 wickets at 29.25, his best performance being 9 for 70 in the Leicestershire v. Kent match at Grace Road in 1985.

First playing in 1984, Philip Whitticase took over as regular wicketkeeper in 1986. Unlucky with injuries, he suffered a badly broken finger which kept him out of most of the 1990 season. After 1991, he lost his place to Paul Nixon. Returning in an emergency for the first match of the 1995 season at Chelmsford, he lost sight of a ball in poor light whilst batting and had seven teeth knocked out. Phil Whitticase caught 309, stumped 14 and made one century – 114 not out against Hampshire at Bournemouth in 1991.

Seven

Present Times

LEICESTERSHIRE v NORTHAMPTONSHIRE

BRITANNIC ASSURANCE CHAMPIONSHIP
JULY 14,15,16 & 17 1998
Grace Road,Leicester
Toss won by Northants who elected to bat
UMPIRES: B Leadbeater & A G T Whitehead
SCORERS: G A York & A Kingston
Next Home Game:July 24 to 27 v **SRI LANKA**

Today's match hosts:

PLEASE NOTE: THE AXA LEAGUE GAME V
NORTHAMPTONSHIRE IS ON SATURDAY
18th JULY AND WILL START AT 2:00 PM

Leicestershire 1st Innings / 2nd Innings

#	Batsman	1st dismissal		1st R	2nd dismissal		2nd R
1	V J Wells	LBW	b Rose	1	c Malcolm b Taylor		58
2	D L Maddy	c Penberthy b Malcolm		3	Run Out		15
3	I J Sutcliffe	c Ripley	b Malcolm	1	b Rose		12
4	B F Smith	c Ripley	b Taylor	153	LBW b Rose		6
5	P V Simmons		b Rose	7	c Penberthy b Rose		25
6	A Habib		Run Out	198	not out		7
7	P A Nixon X	c Ripley	b Rose	27	Run Out		2
8	C C Lewis *	c Bailey	b Rose	8	not out		71
9	D J Millns	c Taylor	b Rose	20			...
10	A D Mullally	c Warren	b Taylor	0			...
11	M T Brimson		not out	18			...
12	C Crowe						
		Extras		48	Extras		8
		Total		484 all out	Total		204

Fall of wickets
1 - 1 2 - 2 3 - 29 4 - 278 5 - 356 6 - 364 7 - 376 8 - 418 9 - 418 10 - 484
1 - 60 2 - 98 3 - 99 4 - 114 5 - 118 6 - 167 7 - 8 - 9 - 10 -

BOWLING	O	M	R	W	BOWLING	O	M	R	W
Malcolm	25	2	113	2	Malcolm	1	0	16	0
Rose	28.2	.1	123	5	Rose	9.1	0	93	3
Curran	10	3	22	0	Taylor	9	0	91	1
Taylor	34	9	75	2					
Swann	13	2	56	0					
Penberthy	15	2	50	0					
Bailey	11	2	21	0					

Northamptonshire 1st Innings / 2nd Innings

#	Batsman	1st dismissal		1st R	2nd dismissal		2nd R
1	R J Warren		b Mullally	5	c Nixon b Mullally		2
2	R J Bailey	c Simmons b Mullally		5	c Lewis b Millns		29
3	M B Loye	c Wells	b Maddy	76	c Lewis b Brimson		19
4	D J Sales		b Mullally	5	c Smith b Mullally		10
5	K M Curran *		b Wells	18	c Sutcliffe b Mullally		18
6	A L Penberthy	c Habib	b Mullally	18	c Nixon b Millns		17
7	G P Swann	c Nixon	b Millns	92	c Sutcliffe b Brimson		111
8	D Ripley X	c Nixon	b Mullally	10	c Simmons b Lewis		32
9	F Rose		b Brimson	1	c Mullally b Brimson		5
10	J P Taylor	c Nixon	b Lewis	41	LBW b Mullally		56
11	D E Malcolm		not out	14	not out		4
12	A J Swann						
		Extras		37	Extras		62
		Total		322 all out	Total		365

Fall of Wickets
1 - 11 2 - 14 3 - 28 4 - 69 5 - 110 6 - 124 7 - 235 8 - 274 9 -275 10 -322
1 - 12 2 - 63 3 - 81 4 - 89 5 - 117 6 - 128 7 - 205 8 - 347 9 -361 10 -365

BOWLING	O	M	R	W	BOWLING	O	M	R	W
Mullally	18	3	62	5	Mullally	27.1	9	48	4
Millns	19	4	61	1	Millns	28	4	83	2
Wells	11	2	45	1	Wells	4	1	8	0
Lewis	14.5	1	73	1	Lewis	23	3	82	1
Brimson	16	5	55	1	Brimson	51	23	88	3
Maddy	3	0	19	1	Maddy	3	0	15	0

This match appeared to be heading for a draw as Leicestershire were set 204 in 20 overs. However, the team had other ideas, and went for it! They recorded the fastest ever innings of over 200 runs in first-class cricket – excepting any achievements in contrived circumstances. The first over went for 16 runs as Vince Wells smashed 58 off 32 balls, whilst Chris Lewis hit 71 from 33 balls. They made the total with five balls to spare!

Timothy James Boon scored 11,821 runs (average 31.35), all of which were for Leicestershire, between 1980 and 1992. Following a serious car accident in South Africa he missed the whole of the 1985 season and played throughout 1986 with a foot-long metal pin in his thigh. He now coaches the England under-19s.

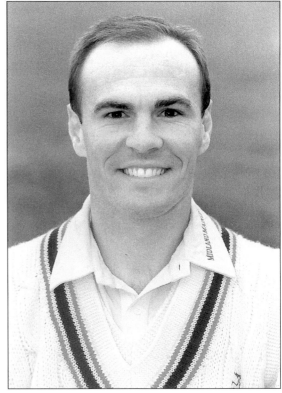

Paul Nixon, born in Carlisle, kept wicket for the county from 1989 to 1999. He has joined Kent for the 2000 season. His aggressive left-handed batting has to date brought 6,269 runs (average 31.03), with 11 centuries. He has taken 469 catches and made 40 stumpings. An ebullient and enthusiastic player, Nico was selected for the England 'A' team tour of India in 1994/95 and is considered unlucky not to have gained senior honours.

The Leicestershire playing staff and officials, 1991. Seated on the front row are, from left to right: Gordon Parsons, Jack Birkenshaw (manager), John Josephs (chairman), Nigel Briers (captain), Charles Palmer (president), James Whitaker, Mike Turner (chief executive), Tim Boon and Peter Willey.

Vincent Wells came from Kent in 1992, after failing to establish a regular place there. He soon developed into an attacking opening batsman, while his medium-pace deliveries have the knack of breaking partnerships. To date he has scored 7,159 runs (average 34.25) and taken 220 wickets at 26.53 each. The highest of his three double centuries (plus another in the NatWest Trophy) is 224 against Middlesex at Lord's in 1997. Taking over as captain when James Whitaker was forced to retire during last season, he has been confirmed in this office for 2000.

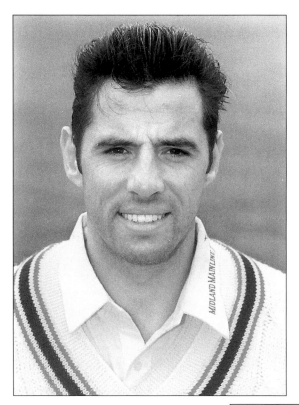

David Millns, a right-arm fast bowler, arrived in 1990 after two seasons with Nottinghamshire. He soon registered his presence, achieving a remarkable analysis of 9 for 37 at Derby in 1991 and in the following year 74 wickets at 20.62 saw him in fifth place in the national bowling averages. His batting has improved to the extent that he has posted three centuries since 1996. Appearing very little in 1999 (his benefit year), David has been released from his contract and has rejoined Nottinghamshire.

Alan Mullally was Millns' opening partner throughout the 1990s. An extremely accurate left-arm seamer, he has been a perfect foil. Now seemingly established in the England side, he has taken 499 wickets at 30 runs each (to the end of the 1999 season). A genuine number eleven batsman, he was born in Southend and spent most of his early life in Australia. Alan has joined Hampshire on a three year contract from 2000.

Play in progress during the Glamorgan match at Grace Road in 1993. Vince Wells is the batsman preparing to take strike. Dickie Bird is umpiring from the bowler's end. The (then) new indoor school building is in the background.

A stylish right-hander, Ben Smith worked his way through the Leicestershire Young Cricketers teams and represented England under-19s in 1991. He made his debut for the county in 1990, aged eighteen, and to date has made 6,698 runs at 36.60. His magnificent innings of 204 at The Oval in the final match of the 1998 season helped to bring the County Championship to Leicestershire.

Philip Verant Simmons was Leicestershire's immensely popular overseas player in 1994, 1996 and 1998. The missing seasons were due to his selection for the West Indies team. In his first match for Leicestershire, Phil Simmons smashed the county's highest individual innings record, which had stood since 1914, with a monumental 261 off the Northamptonshire attack at Grace Road. The innings contained 34 fours and 4 sixes and required only 354 balls. He has scored 11,394 runs in first-class cricket (at 35.94) and has taken 203 wickets at 29.10. A superb slip fielder, he has held 233 catches in only 200 matches.

A desolate scene at Grace Road following flash flooding a few summers ago. Since then, amongst many other ground improvements, the drains and drainage system have been completely renewed.

Relaying part of the square at Grace Road in September 1995, after a heavy season.

The presentation of the County Championship Cup at Buckingham Palace on 13 November 1996. This solid gold cup is presented by the Lord's Taverners, and it is for this reason that the winners are invited to Buckingham Palace to receive the cup from The Duke of

Edinburgh. Phil Simmons, Alan Mullally, Gordon Parsons, Vince Wells, Ben Smith and Darren Maddy had all returned temporarily from their winter commitments to be present on this occasion.

The 1996 Championship winning team. From left to right, back row: Aftab Habib, Ben Smith, Phil Simmons, Alan Mullally, Adrian Pierson, Gordon Parsons. Front row: Vince Wells, James Whitaker, Paul Nixon, Darren Maddy, David Millns.

The Second XI won the Bain Hogg Trophy for the third time in four successive final appearances on 9 September 1996 when Leicestershire beat Durham by 46 runs at Grace Road (in front of their largest ever crowd for a Second XI match). The victorious squad are, from left to right, back row: Iain Sutcliffe, James Ormond, Tim Mason, Darren Stevens, Dominic Williamson, Vince Clarke, Gregor MacMillan, Steven Bartle. Front row: Craig Mortimer (physiotherapist), Carlos Remy, Phil Whitticase, Phil Robinson (captain), Jon Dakin, Carl Crowe.

Following his long and successful playing career, Jack Birkenshaw was a first-class umpire from 1982 to 1988 and then cricket manager with Somerset from 1989 to 1991. However, his heart was always with Leicestershire and he rejoined the county in 1992 as cricket manager. A good man-manager, with an eye for talent, he has made some astute signings and was instrumental in building the successful Leicestershire teams of the 1990s. He scored 12,780 runs and took 1,073 wickets in his playing career, which lasted from 1958 to 1981.

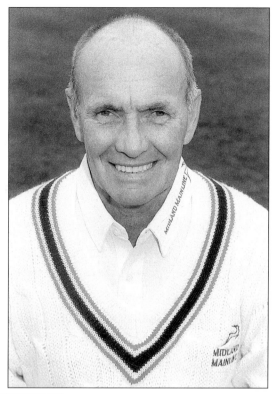

The other half of 'The Management', James Whitaker was appointed captain in 1996 and led the team to two Championships in three years. He fired up the players with his infectious enthusiasm, always leading from the front, and gelled them into a team. He suffered a severe knee injury early in 1998 and did not face a ball in Championship matches, but stayed with the team when he was back on his feet. Unfortunately, this led to his enforced retirement during 1999. Selected once for England, James' career batting record, starting in 1983, is 17,198 runs at 38.56. He has now been appointed secretary/manager of Leicestershire CCC.

James Whitaker shaking hands with E.E. Snow at a lunch at Grace Road during the summer of 1997. Eric Snow was a County Club member of over seventy years' standing who had been housebound for some years due to physical incapacity. The club brought him to the ground for this occasion, which gave him great pleasure. He had been librarian for over forty years, and a committee member for thirty, being elected a vice-president in 1983 for his long and valuable service. Sadly, Eric died in September 1998, in his eighty-ninth year.

Darren Maddy earned his first Test cap against New Zealand at The Oval in the summer of 1999, having been on the 'A' team tours in the previous two winters. He was selected for the England tour of South Africa in the winter of 1999/2000. A right-handed opening batsman, he made his debut for Leicestershire in 1994, in which season he scored a record total of 1,498 runs in the Second XI Championship. Darren has made over 5,000 runs in first-class cricket, with a highest score of 202 for England 'A' v. Kenya in 1997/98.

Aftab Habib played once for Middlesex in 1992, but was released, and joined Leicestershire in 1995. An elegant right hander, he played in the first two Tests against New Zealand in the summer of 1999 and has been successful with the 'A' team in Bangladesh and New Zealand during the winter. His best score is 215 against Worcestershire at Grace Road in 1996.

Iain Sutcliffe obtained boxing blues at Oxford in 1993 and 1994 and cricket blues in 1995 and 1996. He first played for the county in 1995 and was capped in 1997. A left hander, the highest of his five hundreds to date is 167 in 1998 against Middlesex at Grace Road.

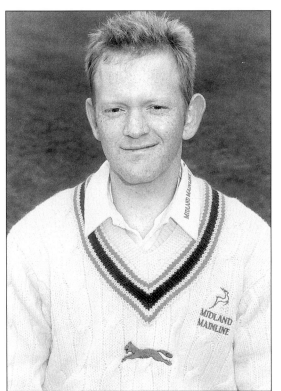

Matthew Brimson joined the Leicestershire staff in 1993 and made his debut in the same year. A slow left-arm bowler, he was capped in 1998. He is also a stubborn tail-end batsman, often used as a nightwatchman. His best bowling return to date was 5 for 12 against Sussex at Grace Road in 1996.

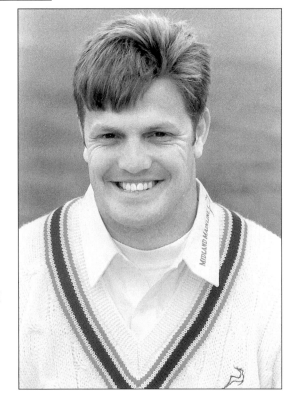

Born in Hitchin, Jonathan Dakin made his debut for the county in 1993. A hard hitting left-hand batsman and right-arm medium-pace bowler, he has not yet cemented a place in the team, despite some useful scores, in particular 190 at Northampton in 1997. More use was made of his bowling in 1999.

James Ormond played one match in 1995 at the age of eighteen and was a member of the England under-19s that season. Missing out the following season, he burst on the scene in 1997, with 44 wickets at 24.11, earning a place in the England 'A' tour that winter. A right-arm fast bowler, he took 52 wickets in 1999.

A full-blooded pull from Karen Smithies. Karen, a left-handed bat and slow right-arm bowler, was captain of the England women's team for several years. During the summer of 1999, she scored her first one-day international century, with 110 not out against India at Trent Bridge. Making her debut in 1987, she has played in 15 Test matches. Karen received an OBE for her services to women's cricket in the 1994 New Year's Honours, having led England to success in the 1993 World Cup. She is now a member of the enthusiastic sales and marketing team at Grace Road.

BRITANNIC ASSURANCE CHAMPIONSHIP
SURREY COUNTY CRICKET CLUB
v
LEICESTERSHIRE COUNTY CRICKET CLUB
on 17th—20th September 1998

Umpires: J.H. Hampshire & K.E. Palmer **Scorers**: K. R. Booth & G.A. York

LEICESTERSHIRE	FIRST INNINGS		SECOND INNINGS
1. D.L. Maddy	c Stewart b Bicknell	7	
2. V.J. Wells	c Salisbury b B. Hollioake	24	
3. I.J. Sutcliffe	c Brown b Benjamin	18	
4. B.F. Smith	c Brown b Shahid	204	
5. P.V. Simmons*	b B. Hollioake	21	
6. A. Habib	c Stewart b B. Hollioake	114	
7. P.A. Nixon†	not out	101	
8. C.C. Lewis	not out	54	
9. D.J. Millns			
10. A.D. Mullally			
11. M.T. Brimson			

EXTRAS   B   lb14   w14   nb14   42   B   lb   w   nb

TOTAL(180 overs for 6 dec)   585   TOTAL

FALL OF WICKETS

First Innings

1	2	3	4	5	6	7	8	9	10
11	44	74	102	354	480				

Second Innings

1	2	3	4	5	6	7	8	9	10

Bowling	O	M	R	W	Wd	Nb	Bowling	O	M	R	W	Wd	Nb
Bicknell	13	4	49	1	....	1							
Benjamin	27	5	95	1	....	....							
B Hollioake	27	3	106	3	2	3							
Butcher	16	3	59	0	3	....							
Salisbury	36	6	111	0	2	....							
A Hollioake	13	2	29	0	....	....							
Amin	39	8	89	0	....	3							
Shahid	7	1	31	1									
Brown	2	1	2	0									

The scorecard of the match which sealed the County Championship for Leicestershire in 1998. This was a superb example of the county's famed teamwork, in which everyone played their part.

SURREY	FIRST INNINGS		SECOND INNINGS	
1. M.A. Butcher	c Maddy b Mullally	0	c Wells b Millns	24
2. A.J. Stewart†	b Lewis	33	c Nixon b Simmons	16
3. Nadeem Shahid	c Nixon b Millns	0	b Simmons	34
4. G.P. Thorpe	lbw b Mullally	0	run out	2
5. A.D. Brown	lbw b Millns	3	st Nixon b Brimson	12
6. A.J. Hollioake*	c Nixon b Lewis	40	not out	54
7. B.C. Hollioake	not out	46	c Millns b Mullally	17
8. I.D.K. Salisbury	lbw b Wells	1	lbw b Simmons	1
9. M.P. Bicknell	c Nixon b Wells	0	c sub b Brimson	31
10. J.E. Benjamin	b Brimson	12	b Millns	0
11. R.M. Amin	c Nixon b Simmons	0	st Nixon b Brimson	12
EXTRAS	B4 lb 3 w nb4	11	B lb11 w4 nb10	25
	TOTAL (43 overs)	146	TOTAL(72.4 overs)	228.

FALL OF WICKETS

	First Innings										Second Innings									
	1	2	3	4	5	6	7	8	9	10	1	2	3	4	5	6	7	8	9	10
	0	0	0	8	40	80	85	85	133	146	47	53	56	85	106	122	123	194	195	228

Bowling	O	M	R	W	Wd	Nb	Bowling	O	M	R	W	Wd	Nb
Mullally	10	4	26	2	....	....	Mullally	20	9	54	1	....	....
Millns	9	3	36	2	....	....	Lewis	4	0	9	0	....	....
Wells	6	2	11	2	....	....	Millns	13	5	32	2	....	....
Lewis	6	1	12	2	....	....	Brimson	21.4	6	62	3	....	.....
Brimson	6	1	33	1	....	....	Simmons	14	3	50	3	....	....
Simmons	6	1	21	1	....	.....							

The fifth-wicket stand of 252 by Ben Smith and Aftab Habib is the county record against Surrey. This was Leicestershire's sixth successive win – the last five producing maximum points.

The new electronic scoreboard at Grace Road was completed for the beginning of the 1999 season. This was financed by the generosity of the Hawkes family, in memory of John Hawkes, a vice-president of the club and member of the management committee for twenty-six years, who died in March 1997.

A view across the Grace Road ground during the first floodlit match in the CGU National League on 29 June 1999. Yorkshire are the opponents.